COPY 1

S
39
INV 82

Make-Believe

Make-Believe

A Meditation on Individual Philosophy

Edited by
John H Moore

TURNSTONE BOOKS LONDON

Set in Press Roman and printed
by Lowe & Brydone (Printers) Ltd, Thetford, Norfolk.

Contents

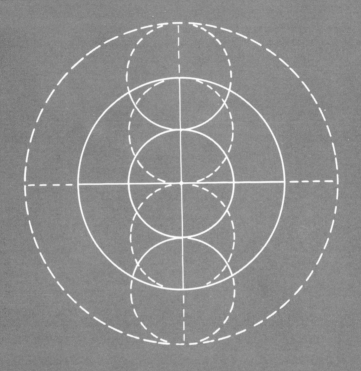

(3)

I   Proposition

This work proposes.

It is a particular interpretation
and its value must lie in its ability to provoke, to "call forth".

It says nothing new;
it puts in a different form what has already been said
in many ways throughout human history. (*1*)

It suggests a direction
for an exploration that each must make for himself.

Words call forth and give form;
the patterns in which the forms crystallise
depend on a man's observation of his own experience;
a different assembly of words
can provoke a re-assessment of experience.

The teachings of the past give instruction, give structure;
they do not by themselves guarantee rejection of ignorance;
they do not tell the truth but they can call forth the Truth; (*2*)
they illuminate and confirm realisation.
They are evidence, not proof.

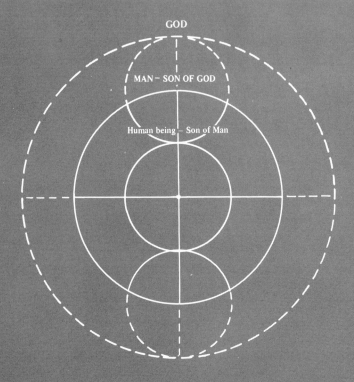

The unmoved human being is as unaware of his evolutionary
possibilities
as a caterpillar might be said to be unaware that it may become a
butterfly. *(4)*
There can be no prediction as to when and how a human being may
spiritually evolve.
In that all humans are given the potential to evolve, so they are equal;
but in the degrees to which they have evolved they are not equal.

In that no human can decide when or how the evolution will take place,
it is never appropriate for him to believe himself superior or
inferior to another,
any more than a butterfly would be justified in believing itself
superior to a caterpillar.

In human evolution, whether he be aware of it or not,
the human being, the humus or ground of being,
must evolve to become Man.
The study and practice of philosophy is the medium
through which the process takes place. *(5)*

The particular human being, a man,
born the Son of Man,
comes to believe in a world of duality and multiplicity; *(6)*
in earning his Manhood,
he becomes unified as Individual Man, *(7)*
the Son of God.

III   *God*

In his learning,
there is introduced to the mind of the human being
the 'god' concept,
a concept to explain the creator of the creation
in which the being has become embodied.

For a long time, it is a case of belief in
'me' and 'god' (duality)
or, for the atheist, 'me' and 'no god' (also duality). (*8*)

The evolution of the human being
lies in the gradual realisation
that 'me' is an illusion,
an assumption,
a non-entity. (*9*)

Realising that there is no 'me',
the duality of 'me' and 'god' dissolves in the mind's acceptance
that there is only God (unity),
not as a vague belief
but as being everything,
indivisible,
Individual.

In this realisation,
a man becomes Man, (*10*)
made in the image of God. (*11*)

When and where to begin an introduction?
Now and here, without reference to past and future.

Beginnings and endings are *in* time, not *of* time;
for who knows the beginning and ending of time?
The beginning and ending of time is an assumption;
there is no comprehensible beginning and ending of time.

A circle has no beginning and ending
and therefore time may best be considered a circle or cycle.
Within the cycle of time, all beginnings and endings co-exist. (*12*)

For example, a man believing in terms of passing time
assumes sunrise to be followed by sunset to be followed by sunrise and
so on;
yet, in reality, the sun never rises nor sets;
it shines all the time.
Somewhere there is sunrise and somewhere there is sunset,
co-existing together.
Likewise, all beginnings and endings co-exist;
they only appear separate from a relative point of view.

The cycle of time, eternity, has no motion itself.
It does not pass; things happen in it.
A beginning is an ending and an ending a beginning.
That which is after the beginning is also before the ending;
and that which is before the beginning is also after the ending.

Passing time is an illusion
arising from the motion of one thing relative to another.
For the one indivisible totality,
the eternal universe,
there can be no illusion of passing time
because, being total, there is no other with which its motion can be
compared.
Appreciation of the motionless time, eternity,
is in the present moment, now and here. (*13*)

An introduction
is a point in time, here and now,
belonging to the present,
independent of imaginary past and future,
past and future belonging to the illusion of passing time.
The present does not belong to the illusion of passing time;
for how long is the present?
For what period in between past and future does the present last?
No time at all.

In the illusion of passing time,
where the motion of a particular thing
has a relationship with the motion of another particular thing,
a caterpillar may become *a* butterfly:
they appear to be separated by passing time.
In the moment now,
belonging to eternity,
the form Caterpillar and the form Butterfly,
whether manifest or unmanifest,
eternally co-exist.

6

In the illusion of passing time,
the question "Which comes first, the chicken or the egg?"
can never be answered.
In the moment now, belonging to eternity,
the once-upon-a-time,
the form Chicken and the form Egg eternally co-exist.

A particular introduction to Individual Philosophy
belongs to a particular point in the space of time, now.
The Individual Philosophy itself belongs to eternity,
beyond passing time.

An introduction is only an introduction,
a leading from the particular into the total.
An introduction to Individual Philosophy
is not the Individual Philosophy itself. (*14*)
The Philosophy itself has to be experienced and realised
by the Individual, (*15*)
free of the belief in a relative existence.
The evidence is here and now,
not in history or speculation.

v *Interpretation*

An introduction to Individual Philosophy,
by means of the spoken or written word,
is an interpretation,
a particular interpretation by a particular human being
according to the particular experience of that being.

A speaker or writer makes a particular interpretation
born of his particular experience,
translating that experience into words as best he can.
The listener or reader
makes a particular interpretation of the original interpretation
according to his particular experience.

At the level of sensorily perceived objects,
those particular interpretations,
for the purposes of communication in the sensorily perceived world,
apparently coincide.
Hence, when the word 'bread' is used,
two persons, speaking the same acquired language,
visualise a similar object.
At this level, with variable efficiency,
the human being, as a sensorily perceivable object,
functions in relation to all other objects
in the sensorily perceivable world.
But,
at a level other than that of the sensorily perceived world,
there can be no certainty that interpretations do coincide.

For example, when the word 'consciousness' is used,
it is not possible for one person to convey to another
exactly what he 'inwardly' experiences as consciousness.
Each must realise for himself what such a word means
in his *own* experience. (*16*)
One can give another bread;
one cannot give another consciousness.

One person cannot tell another what consciousness *is*
because of the limitations of the spoken and written word.
The impossibility arises from the fact that,
in order to describe an abstract experience,
abstract words have to be used
('abstract' here meaning
that which is other than sensorily perceived
or describable in terms of the sensorily perceived world).
And how could it be possible to define the abstract words
needed in order to define the abstract? (*17*)
Consciousness cannot be defined nor described
because it does not have the properties and limitations
of a sensorily perceived object.
It is not possible to describe what consciousness *is*.(*18*)
All confusion in philosophy and religion
is due to one adopting the interpretation of another,
or rejecting the interpretation of another,
forgetting that *experience* of the indefinable and indescribable
cannot be conveyed by the spoken and written word.

The fact that the forms of religion and philosophy
are only interpretations tends to be forgotten;
the maintenance, propagation and destruction of interpretations
becomes an end in itself.

The purpose of religion and philosophy
is not to persuade or manipulate one
to believe in another's interpretation and assertion,
but to guide each one to observe and interpret
his own experience;
to liberate him, in fact, from the interpretation of others.
Their purpose is not to inculcate belief (*19*)
but to liberate from false belief.

The failure of religion and philosophy
is that they become a substitute,
deflecting a man from his responsibility,
responsibility here being the ability to respond,
the ability to observe and answer to his own experience. (*20*)

For example, it is possible for a man to say:
"I believe in God";
but only he can know what he means by the statement.
He certainly cannot tell another what it means to him as an experience.

If someone asks: "Do you believe in God?"
the appropriate answer must be:
"First you tell me what you mean by 'God' ".
And if one asks another to believe in his interpretation or assertion
of the indescribable and indefinable,
he asks the impossible.
For one cannot truthfully believe, be free,
in the interpretation or assertion of another.
If he trusts that another's interpretation or assertion
is reliable evidence of the indefinable, he is deluded.
He must convince himself through his own experience. (*21*)

For, at the level of 'bread',
there are other people;
at the level 'consciousness',
there are no other people.
There are many loaves of bread and many people;
but how many consciousnesses are there?

At a level other than that of the sensorily perceived world
one person cannot be said truthfully to comprehend
the experience of another
in that
one person cannot experience the experience of another.
Two persons cannot be in the same place simultaneously.

Particular speaks to particular, a part to a part;
the Individual,
that which cannot be divided,
cannot speak to another
because He is One and Alone, All-One.

Can one person do another's dying for him?
It is not possible for 'me' to convince 'you'
that 'you' do not die;
but it is possible for a man to convince himself
and to understand that He does not die. (*22*)

There is limitation in any philosophical interpretation.
The interpreter is limited in that he must use words
in an attempt to define and describe
and the receiver then has to make an interpretation
of that interpretation,
attempting to understand what the originator means.

There is therefore need for caution. (*23*)
The speaker or author and the listener or reader
must be constantly mindful of this insuperable limitation.
Each must exercise discipline,
that of always being a disciple, one who needs to learn.

The speaker or writer must use words with care,
realising that he cannot describe Truth,
only attempt to guide by demonstrating the un-true or false;
and the listener or reader
must neither accept nor reject any proposal
until he has put it honestly to the test of his own experience, (*24*)
experience being that which reveals itself in any given moment.

For it is not until a man begins to observe his own experience,
free from indiscriminately acquired assumptions,
that he can realise what is undeniable. (*25*)

Words lead the mind into ignorance;
they also have the power to demonstrate that ignorance. (*26*)
The mind led out of ignorance
dis-covers Truth.

In the beginning was the Word. (*27*)
The Truth is 'before' the beginning,
that which speaks the Word in the first place.

Ultimately, a person can only discover what is undeniable
through observation of his own experience, (*28*)
each person's experience telling him
precisely what he needs to know. (*29*)
And this is not possible whilst the mind is occupied
with beliefs adopted, assumptions made and opinions formed
indiscriminately
which is to say, adopted, made and formed unquestioningly
without the exercise of reason.

Philosophy might be described as the examination of belief,
for what a man believes is his philosophy. (*30*)
Every man is a philosopher
in that every sane (healthy) man comes to believe in something
and what a man believes is the truth for him.
To believe in something is to have faith in it or to trust it
as seeming constant or reliable.
A philosophy is essentially
the beliefs under which a man conducts himself,
since his beliefs usually rule and regulate his actions.

There are those who learn the interpretations of others,
compare and contrast the interpretations of others
and postulate their own interpretations
without reference to their own experience.
They thereby confine philosophy to a theoretical study
which has no practical significance.

And there are those who develop haphazard 'personal' philosophies
born of their varied experiences in the sensorily perceived world.
These 'personal' philosophies,crude and limited though they may be,
serve the conduct of their day to day activities.
They are practical but, since they change with circumstances,
and since they are therefore partial and inconsistent,
and, as such, not lastingly reliable,
they are of little value to others,
nor, ultimately, of any deep value to themselves.

The former might be likened to those who have many theories
as to how to make bread but have no experience of actually making it
and the latter to those who attempt to make bread
without proper instruction
and therefore produce an unsatisfactory and unsatisfying result.

There are many philosophies and religions
and hence confusion, conflict and little common understanding. (*31*)
The evolution of the human being
depends on his admitting that his *acquired* beliefs
are unreasonable, inconstant and fundamentally unreliable.

If he admits to the incompleteness and unreliability
of his particular philosophy,
he will seek to discover one that is complete and reliable. (*32*)
It is proposed that there is, always has been and always will be
one Individual Philosophy,
from which has stemmed all teachings and religions,
all teachings and religions being particular interpretations
of that one inexpressible, innate, Individual Philosophy.

A philosophy is based on acquired beliefs;
The one Individual Philosophy is innate in each human being.
It is discovered through Love of Knowledge
and leads to Knowledge of Love.

VIII   *Responsibility*

The one Individual Philosophy has been interpreted
through the spoken and written word in different languages
at different points in the cycle of time,
on each occasion in a manner appropriate to the state of humanity.
It reveals the answers to the important questions
innate in each human being.

Among the most important questions pondered by the human mind
are:
"What is man?",
"What is the universe?"
"How are the two related?"
The realisation of the answers to these questions is Knowledge.

Considering these fundamental questions
is another aspect of philosophy,
and the ability of the human mind to consider them
is its most important responsibility. (*33*)
All the rest is a dream.
Upon this responsibility all other responsibilities depend,
for until it is Known what Man is, what the Universe is
and how the two are related,
the mind cannot Know fully what Responsibility means.

Responsibility means the ability to respond.
To what is the human mind responsible?
To what does it respond?

If the mind is permitted to consider such questions,
it is understood that without such Knowledge
living is irresponsible and apparently meaningless. (*34*)

It is frequently said in so many words,
"No one has ever found the answers."
This is because, through education, we have become accustomed
to finding answers 'out there' in the world
and no one has ever found the answers there.
The answers are 'within'
and can only be revealed by looking 'within'
to dis-cover what has really been Known always,
especially as a child.

The law is however that it is impossible to tell others
partly because the relating of experience
can never transfer the experience to another
but mainly because the experience reveals that
there are no others to tell.

Accepting responsibility then
is answering to the Knowledge 'within'.
As surely as the important questions arise from 'within'
so are they answered 'within'.
The going out and the returning are a lifetime's work.

IX   *Knowledge*

Any man who ignores the responsibility
of endeavouring to find the answers to the important questions
is ignorant, (*35*)
an *ignorant* man being one who *ignores*.
All normal human beings ask these questions,
'normal' here meaning one capable of development,
but, because they fail to find satisfactory guidance
or because of involvement in worldly affairs,
they remain ignorant. (*36*)

The realisation of the answers to the important questions
is Knowledge,
Knowledge being Realisation of the Real.
All the rest that is called knowledge
is learning or knowing *about* things (about = around).
Knowledge becomes buried in learning.
Learning is introduced to the mind after physical birth;
Knowledge is present always,
like the heart knowing how to beat or a flower how to grow,
and it is quite other than knowing about things.

Real Knowledge, Knowledge of the Real, the Regal, is not learned;
it is already there 'within'.
The uncovering of it, the realising it, the making it real,
is the purpose of philosophy, the purpose of man.

The heart or spring of *Kno*wledge is Now; *(37)*
and the heart or spring of No*w* is O.

Real Knowledge is 'within';
it is always available to this creation whilst there is Human Being.
But it is *for-gotten*;
learning is *got* in exchange *for* Knowledge,
whereas learning about things should be the complement
in existence of Knowledge.

Knowledge remains hidden 'within'
so long as the mind pursues learning about things alone
in the belief and assumption that learning about things
is able to provide the answers to the important questions; *(38)*
and so long as the mind is set continually in pursuit
of pleasure and comfort in the belief and assumption
that pleasure and comfort provide lasting happiness.
So long as the mind ignores what is Known,
no matter how much is learned about the world,
no matter how much pleasure and comfort are found,
the man is never any the wiser as to what he *is*,
what the universe *is*, nor how the two are related.

The real Knowledge has to be re-membered,
the mind has to be re-minded,
for the Knowledge to be re-cognised.

When some truthful statement is encountered,
one that has not been encountered before,
something 'within' recognises it;
it could not be re-cognised (re-known)
unless it were already Known.

Real Knowledge is Conscience (with-knowledge, in-tuition).
Conscience is often in conflict with what has been learned
by a particular mind in a particular time and place.
The conflict between what is Known 'inwardly'
and what has been learned 'externally'
is the conflict of mind.
This is war of mind as opposed to peace of mind
and the resolution of the former into the latter
comes with the realisation of, the emergence of, Knowledge. (*39*)
Reliance on the Undeniable replaces reliance on partial information.

The real Knowledge is in the 'heart' of every human being (*40*)
and it is in this respect that all men are equal.
Inequality amongst men lies in the differing degrees
to which Knowledge is hidden or ignored.
It is for each to un-cover it, dis-cover it
through observation of his own experience (*41*)
guided by truthful interpretations of the Individual Philosophy.
Being the same Knowledge in all men
that have been, are, or ever will be,
there has been, is and always will be only one Individual Philosophy.

Being Known undeniably in the heart,
it is there in potential, waiting to be realised.
It is itself without form, outside form,
but expresses itself in form;
all forms in-form of it.

If he will withdraw a while from the confusion of learning,
if he will rest a while from the pursuit of pleasure and comfort,
if he will refrain for a while from reliance on things 'out there',
if he will observe his own inner experience
and see what that experience reveals,
the Knowledge is restored
and he Knows undeniably. (*42*)

When a man is moved to discover what he is,
he becomes a disciple.
A disciple is one who puts himself under discipline
in order to be educated, led-out-of ignorance,
by the innate Knowledge.
Putting himself under,
standing under Knowledge,
there is under-standing.

The Authority which is under-stood is the Author of the Knowledge;
the Knowledge is constant, standing-with the Author. (*43*)

x   *Education*

The one Individual Philosophy is the Knowledge
what man is, what the universe is, and how the two are related.
Man has always been blessed with this Knowledge,
the birthright that makes Him what He is,
the birthright that is sold for partial knowledge.
It is 'within' each human being, quiescent, when the body is born
and, as he grows up,
when the mind receives a truthful expression of the one Philosophy
through the spoken or written word,
the Knowledge 'within' responds.

Responsibility is to live in response to that Knowledge.
Re-cognition of that Knowledge,
re-knowing that which has been for-gotten,
is the real meaning of Education, the leading out of Ignorance.
What is commonly called education
might better be called induction,
the channelling or feeding into the mind
of information about the names and properties of things.

According to the degree to which the community in which he lives
worships learning or worships sensory pleasure,
so men become more or less ignorant of the one Individual Philosophy.
When it is not sought, it remains hidden.
This is not to suggest that
learning or pleasure should be forsaken or forbidden:
it is simply that,

when they become the total concern of man,
when he believes and assumes that
they are the source of real Knowledge and lasting Happiness, *(44)*
he will never find lasting fulfilment nor contentment.
Learning and pleasure have their place,
but it is a subsidiary or complementary place.

XI Names & Properties

Learning, or knowledge *about* a thing
induces the mistaken belief and assumption
that the name and properties of the thing are what it *is*. *(45)*

Consider an apple.
'Apple' is the name given to a particular object.
It is the name given to it, for the purposes of identification,
in a particular language.
An Englishman says the object is "an apple";
a Frenchman says it is "une pomme";
it cannot *be* two things at once.
These are just the names that have been given to an object.
So, to what have the names been given?
What is an object before you believe it to be what you have learned to
call it?

The object is further classified as a fruit
and described as round, firm, fleshy, many-celled,
red or green or yellow, edible, and so on;
all these are its properties.
But the properties of a thing are what belong to it;
they are not what it *is*;
so, what is that to which these properties belong?
The object cannot *be* the sum total of its properties
but that which possesses the properties.
Looking at the object called "apple",
with a clear, silent and unprejudiced mind,

it is Known that it *is* none of those words that describe it.
That Knowing undeniably is Knowledge.
That Knowing that an object is none of those words which describe it
is Knowledge arising out of experience.
To believe an object *is* what it is called is ignorant
because believing it *is* what it is called
ignores what it really *is*. (*46*)

One who thus contemplates (with-temple, with-open-space),
free of belief, assumption and opinion,
even though he has believed since childhood
that an apple *is* the name he has learned to call it,
realises undeniably, in truthfulness, that that is not what it *is*.
Knowing undeniably further,
that it is not known what in reality the object *is*,
is to move away from ignorance towards Wisdom,
Realisation of the Real.
The prelude to Wisdom is to realise that it is not Known
what anything *is*. (*47*)

For the purposes of communication and conduct
in the sensorily perceived world,
it is necessary to learn concerning the names and properties
of particular objects.
But it is ignorant to believe that it can be learned
what in reality those objects are.
In order to realise what a thing *is*,
it is necessary to give up believing
that it is what one has learned and assumed it to be.

If a thing is neither its name nor its properties, what is it?
It is not possible to know what a thing is because it *is* Knowledge.

XII *Body-Image as the Self*

The ignorance which surrounds, or is super-imposed upon,
real Knowledge has been likened to a cloud or fog
and it is formed of the accumulated assumptions,
based on haphazard beliefs
picked up at random from various sources
throughout the current physical existence.
Chief amongst misleading beliefs are those which give rise
to the mistaken and limiting assumptions
which a man *makes about* himself.

They are chief amongst misleading beliefs because, in turn,
they lead to a misleading and limiting view of the universe,
and hence to a multitude of mistaken, and ultimately useless,
attitudes and opinions. *(48)*
The ideas encountered,
which through interpretation become particular concepts,
which then through adoption become particular beliefs,
which then become established as habitual assumptions,
giving rise in turn to a pattern of attitudes and opinions,
will be those held in a particular time and place,
the time and place of the current embodiment.

Why should one belief be adopted in preference to another?
Why should beliefs be adopted at all?

Since the power of discrimination does not operate
in the first years or phase of embodiment,
the power of discrimination here being the power of the real
Knowledge or Conscience to reject that which is unreasonable,
the mind will adopt without question
a whole pattern of beliefs introduced to it.
Automatically arising from those beliefs
will be a proliferation of assumptions, attitudes and opinions
under which that mind will thereafter labour.

It is these beliefs, assumptions, attitudes and opinions
which will burden, bind and limit the mind,
which will absorb considerable energy for their maintenance,
which will cause considerable tension
when their validity is contradicted and threatened,
unless and until
the one Individual Philosophy frees the mind of them
and reveals the freedom of the state of pure Believing.

As long as the mind possesses beliefs,
the mind is possessed.
There is trusting in assumption.

Consider one of the principal beliefs,
that which in great part leads a man to assume what he is.
A baby lies awake receiving impressions through the senses;
he cannot,
because the operation of memory and the accumulation of learning
have hardly begun,
interpret the impressions being received.

There is, for that being, just
hearing, touching, seeing, tasting, smelling,
but no interpretation as to what is
heard, touched, seen, tasted, smelled.
He does not name anything.
He does not think he knows what anything is.
He does not have a concept of himself.
He *is*; but does not Know that he is (innocent).

For him there is no concept of himself
nor interpretation of what is sensed.
There is no separation, no thinking being separate.
He and the universe are not believed to be separate.
There simply *is* what *is*, as a unified whole.
For the baby, then, there is no duality conceived,
no concept of himself as an entity being distinct
from what is being sensed.
If he could express himself,
he might say "I am" *or* "There is".

As the memory begins to record experience,
that which 'appears-out-of' the current physical existence,
he begins to *take interest*,
from the capital investment of his being.
He begins to become involved, turned-into,
and as if by magic *is* turned into,
the sensory impressions being received.
Associations are formed
and he gives meaning according to his learning.

Those who care for him and come into contact with him speak to him
as though he *is* the body into which he has been born.
In this way, he acquires the belief and makes the assumption
that he *is* the body, (*49*)
or, better, the body-image.
The belief takes root and grows as the assumption
that he is that body-image created from sensory impressions.
Thus *he creates himself*.
Likewise, he assumes that other body-images are 'other people'
because in the speech he hears
he comes to associate 'me' and 'you'
with his body-image and another body-image.
Assuming that other body-images are 'other people'
the belief is held and the assumption made
that he is one amongst a multitude.
Assuming them all entities,
invested with particular names and properties,
he creates them all.

At the same time,
he hears certain forms given particular names.
To meet the need to identify
and to differentiate one form from another,
he associates particular names with particular forms.
The people in his environment have assumed that a thing *is*
what it is called, and the child automatically, by imitation,
falls into the same assumption.
His body-image is given a name
and, when asked, that is who he says he is.
He learns to refer to other people as their body-images
with their particular names.

Holding the belief of himself as his body-image with a particular name,
and other people as being their body-images with their particular
names,
and a multitude of different objects with their different names,
he comes to believe in a multitude of separate entities. (50)
The unified whole experienced by the baby
has become a multitude of divided parts.

Through sensory impressions,
especially sound, touch and sight,
the child acquires a store of information
of the properties of things in relation to his body —
soft, hard, hot, cold, large, small, and so on.
Through the motion of his body, he accepts the concepts of time and
space.

Thus he accepts a concept of the universe
entirely related to his body
and, since he believes himself to be the separate body-image,
he becomes bound to the belief
that the sensorily perceived world is separate from him,
the reality 'out there',
the place where he is and where he belongs.

He does not realise
that the whole assumption as to what he is,
and what the universe is,
has been entirely fabricated,
created under the spell of acquired belief.
The belief in there being both himself *and* the universe is a fiction
a MAKE–BELIEVE.

Believing himself to be his body-image,
— who is the 'he' to whom the body-image belongs? —
and believing in a universe related to that body-image,
he assumes himself separate
from that which is apparently providing the experience,
a thing separate from all other things.
A fundamental, 'deep-in-the-mind', duality is established.
For him, the reality appears to be
himself the centre, surrounded by the universe.
In Reality, such an assumption is not reasonable.

In this picture, he assumes himself to be more or less a constant;
yet what is constant?
The body and the contents of mind are changing continuously;
they are continuously dependent on the in-flow and out-flow
of substances and impressions;
they could not exist, would not be, without their environment. (*51*)
The belief in himself as a constant and separate entity
is, upon examination and reflection, untenable.

All this super-imposition is a quantum jump from the beginning
when, as a baby, there was no concept of duality nor multiplicity,
just unity unknown and unrealised.
Whereas it was then 'I am' *or* 'There is'
now there is 'me' *and* 'that', 'me' *and* 'all those'.
Forsaking the state of pure unified Being, (*52*)
a fall that seems unavoidable in this creation,
a man becomes almost totally involved,
bound in the belief in himself as a separate entity
surrounded by the entity universe. (*53*)

Having taken this path,
he assumes himself to have been born when the body was born
and he assumes that he dies when the body dies;
when there is pain, he believes he is in pain;
he becomes subject to all the laws that flesh is heir to.
He falls into ignorance,
and, in this state of involvement, he sleeps, (54)
forgetting what He really *is*.
The important questions come to mind to wake him;
he tries to answer them within his concept of reality (corpo-reality)(55)
and they are not answered.
His concept of himself as the body-image,
and of the universe related to his body-image,
will never answer them.

In order to remember what He really *is*,
the mind needs to be 'loosened',
liberated from the limitations of primitive concepts,
acquired beliefs, blind assumptions and valueless opinions.
He must 'come out of what he is not'. (56)

It is Known 'within' undeniably
that in reality he is not the body-image; (57)
the body is a vehicle and a tool for use in this time and place.
It is Known 'within' undeniably
that in reality he is not the contents of mind;
these contents are the agents through which the process
of creation, maintenance and dissolution take place.
Hence, one of the cardinal injunctions is "Know Thy Self",
the One to whom the body and the contents of mind belong. (58)

The "fall", or the original sin,
is the for-getting and the forsaking by man of what he really *is*,
with its complement, the assuming himself to be that which he is not.
The great and fundamental mis-take
is the coming to believe himself to be the body-image,
for upon that assumption depends his view of the world
and his relationship to it: (*59*)
and, though for practical purposes,
he has to learn of the laws and the nature of the physical world,
because he has been incarnated,
it is a limiting view because it confines him to a reality
which will never give him lasting fulfilment nor contentment.
It is an ignorant view because it denies or ignores the view
which can enable him to evolve to understanding.

The limited view continually fills the mind with confusion,
which means in this case the fusing or mixing together
of that which is accurate with that which is inaccurate,
of what is really Known with that which has been mistakenly learned.
For the power of discrimination and evaluation
is continually confronted with the problems that arise
from the duality of 'me' and 'that'.
It has to work continually to choose what is best for 'me'
in relation to this or that phenomenon which is separate from 'me',
within the context of acquired beliefs as to what is beneficial
and what is disadvantageous for 'me'.
Anxiety and tension arise in the mind, projecting distortion in the body,
because the universe continually fails to make provision
for the requirements that 'me' makes upon it.

A continual war rages between 'ought' and 'ought not';
what ought to happen and ought not to happen,
what 'me' ought to do and ought not to do,
what 'me' ought to have and ought not to have;
a destructive, futile and never-ending war. (*60*)

This *occupation* of the mind
with the continual problem of 'me' and 'my' place in the world,
the image building of 'me' for 'my' benefit and 'others',
the striving for 'my' comfort and happiness, and so on,
gives rise to inaccurate judgement and selfish action,
a confusing and blinding fog or cloud which denies the mind
its proper functioning in tranquility.
Because the *pre-occupation* with 'me' in relation to 'that'
is at variance with the mind's desire to obey,
the accurate assessment, born of the Knowledge which is present
at the same time, is frequently distorted or ignored.

For example, consider the belief in the possession of things
and the assumption that the possession of things brings happiness.
At the same time as the desire to possess something occupies
the mind, there is the Knowledge that the fulfilment of that
desire to possess will not bring lasting happiness.
For each Knows that, in Reality,
it is not possible to possess anything,
inasmuch as any thing thought to be possessed may be taken away.
How can any thing that at any moment might be taken away
be truly possessed?
Since at any moment any thing can be taken away,
and ultimately certainly will be taken away,
why rely on it to provide happiness?

Accurate and objective assessment
meets the need of the situation,
giving rise to 'clean' action,
without the importation of 'my' judgement of,
or 'my' justification for, the action, either before or after. *(61)*

If the action required by the situation
is modified by the inter-vention, the coming-between, of 'me',
or by the inter-ference, the making-between, of 'me',
that action is rendered selfish.
If an action is free of the machinations
of the false, illusory self,
that action remains self-less,
no matter how it may be judged by others.

It is not appropriate to judge the actions of others
to be selfish or selfless; *(62)*
Apart from the impossibility of doing so with certainty,
what value is it to you to think that you know that another man's
action is selfless or selfish? *(63)*
But it is of great importance to the man himself that he should
be able to observe and assess his own actions and their effects. *(64)*

The intervention and interference by 'me' for 'my' benefit,
especially at the expense of another,
and the permitting of 'my' judgement as to how things ought
or ought not to be,
are both cases of useless disquiet.

xv Discrimination

A concept is the birth in particular mind of an idea,
an idea being neutral, without form, impersonal, universal
and becoming a concept when interpreted in form by a particular mind.
When conceived in particular mind,
the impersonal idea becomes a personal concept
and may then become rooted and grow as a belief
as trust or faith is put into it.
Without discrimination, any belief can become established
and produce a dense foliage of assumption, attitude and opinion.

As the belief thrives and gives rise to assumption,
its power to influence and restrict
deprives the mind of its natural magnanimity.
Occupied with belief, the mind is robbed of its
space for tolerance,
air of inspiration,
water of fluidity or flexibility,
fire of enterprise and light of discovery,
and its earth of common sense and stability.

When the power of discrimination is feeble,
beliefs rule the mind, often in conflict with each other.
Often in mankind,
beliefs are strongly inculcated into the minds of children,
so strongly that their power of discrimination never develops
and they never have the opportunity to choose
whether they would prefer not to adopt those beliefs.

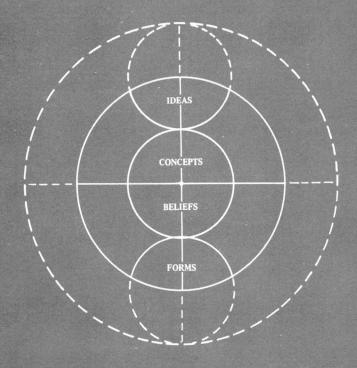

IDEAS

CONCEPTS

BELIEFS

FORMS

The practical aspect of philosophy is the bringing of a man
to observe objectively the beliefs held;
not just the superficial beliefs but those so deep-rooted
that he may not even be aware that he has at some time acquired them,
so established are they as assumptions.

Having observed them,
those beliefs that are found to be unreasonable
may be dislodged by the power of discrimination —
which is the power of innate Knowledge to discern and divide
the appropriate from the inappropriate, the proper from the improper,
the reasonable from the unreasonable, and so on.
Once dislodged, the assumptions, attitudes and opinions dissolve, (65)
hence modifying actions so that they become reasonable.

Belief, trust or faith in all things, in any thing,
is replaced by Belief,
the natural, obedient, clear and peaceful state of mind
of Faith in the Beloved. (66)

To undertake this process of purification, or purgatory,
is to begin to remove the inappropriate beliefs
which confuse and confound the mind
with a cloud of useless imaginings and opinions. (67)
The Knowledge innate is re-leased, realised,
as the organ of discrimination is Educated.

The usefulness of the mind is its emptiness
in the same way that the usefulness of the pot is the space inside.
The conflict of ought and ought not is resolved by nought.

XVI *Identity*

The strength of a belief depends on the degree
to which the being has identified with it,
put trust in its constancy and reliability.
Identify means, here, to make something an entity,
to give something value, to 'entify-the-id',
to give something a witnessed existence as a separate entity.
Something believed, be-loved,
is something that is allowed to assume existence as an entity
through the will or desire of the being.

Purgation is the removal or relinquishing of unreasonable belief.
It means no longer ascribing false values,
no longer trying to make something what 'me' wants it to be.
It means letting all things exist in their own right
with no super-imposition on them of what they mean to 'me'.
Purgatory has gained its connotation of discomfort (*32*)
because it is not easy to withdraw from beliefs
to which one has become attached and given credence.

And that difficulty arises because
the giving of identity to,
and the attachment to,particular beliefs
helps to give the believer his own supposed identity.
By identifying, he creates his own supposed identity.
becoming that with which he has chosen to identify. (*68*)

All things become entities by permission
of he who allows them to be so.

40

If a belief is no longer held, it loses its existence
and, no longer being believed, it disappears,
returning to the unmanifest state
where it no longer has the power to occupy the mind
nor cause its expression in speech and behaviour.
What a man believes is the truth for him; (69)
if, for example, he believes he will die, then he will die.

It is essential that false belief is only properly dissolved
by undeniable Knowledge,
conviction arising out of observation of own experience.
A false belief is one adopted without discrimination
through haphazard learning,
and to have one 'external' learned belief replaced by another
is ultimately useless,
although there are degrees of improvement.
And to have false beliefs removed by 'external' means
without the complementary revelation of inner conviction
is also ultimately useless, even dangerous.

The purpose of practical philosophy
is to reveal that which is undeniably Known 'within'
by the relinquishing of the fiction
that has become super-imposed upon it.
And this can only be done voluntarily by the man's own power of
discrimination, (70)
in his own good time.
It cannot be done any other way because no man can Know for another
any more than he can experience for another,
or become happy by being told to be so.
No man can persuade nor force another to undertake this work;
and no man can do it for another.

XVII

The Self

The basic illusion,
upon which is built all further illusion,
is the belief that one is the sensorily perceived body-image,
mis-taking the experience *of* one-self to *be* one-self.
So what is one-self?
In the first place, in Reality, ONE IS. (*71*)
In the second place, in Creation,
one is that which witnesses creation.
One is that which perceives in preference, (made-before),
to that which is perceived;
which is a reflection of the perceiver;
the perceiver reflecting upon himself.

Supposing someone produces a photograph of 'you' as a child
and says "This is you when you were young".
Is it really believed that that image is or was 'you'?
Is it not Known that the statement is inaccurate?
Is it not impossible to believe that that strange image
is what you were or are?
Perhaps the scene when the photograph was taken is remembered.
The experience of that scene being remembered,
is it not Known that You were looking through the eyes of that child?
Who or what was looking through the eyes of that child?
And is not that which was looking through the eyes of that child
the same as that which is looking out now?

The appearance of the body-image changes,
the contents of the mind alter,
but that which is looking at the sight through the eyes,
that which is watching the changing contents of mind,
has that grown older or changed?
Who or what is there in the black fathomless depth
of the nought in the centre of the eye, out of which there is seeing?

The body is the vehicle through which the creation is perceived
but who or what is doing the perceiving?
What is that which witnesses through the senses?
What is that which witnesses the thoughts and images in the mind?
That Witness is what You Are;
that is the One-Self; (72)
that is the I, the One Eye, the One and Only I. (73)
One is I; I is One.

That which witnesses through the senses is what One is,
the real Self, the real I.
And what can be said of that Self which Witnesses?
What can be said of that which hears through the ears, sees through
the eyes, touches through the skin, and so on?
What is this I? Where is this I?
Since it witnesses all that is describable,
it must itself be indescribable.
If it were describable, there would still then be that, beyond,
which was witnessing in order to be able to describe.
And that would be the Self.
Any thing is describable
since to be a thing it must have qualities and properties
to make it appear as that thing.
It therefore follows that the Self is No Thing. (74)

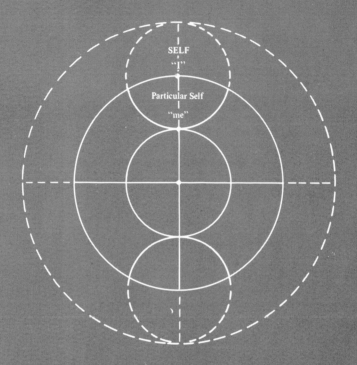

44

Contemplate, in experience, now,
what witnesses through the senses.
Can it be said to have describable form?
What can be said of it?
Whenever there is awareness of any thing, it is there.
It is always the same,
baby, child, youth, man.
It never alters nor decays.
It is not subject to the laws
of the sensorily nor mentally perceived worlds.
All things change
but not that which witnesses the changes.

The Self is that which witnesses the sensory impressions;
the Self is that which witnesses the thoughts and images of mind;
the Self is that which witnesses the dreams of sleep;
and that which witnesses only witnesses.
The Self does nothing, achieves nothing, possesses nothing. (75)
The Self is there in the newly-born baby and in the aged man,
just witnessing all that comes to pass.
That I is the Single Eye of Mind
and the realising, the making real, of that Self is Self-Realisation.

Because the Self has no defineable properties,
the Self is indefineable. (76)
Because it cannot be said how large or how small the Self is,
the Self is limitless and infinite.
Because the Self is formless,
there is only One Self.
Because the Self is One, there is no other with which it can be compared,
and the Self is therefore incomparable.
Because the Self does not alter nor decay and is always the same,

the Self cannot die and is therefore eternal. (77)
Because the Self is formless, the Self cannot be said to have location
and is therefore, at the same time, everywhere and nowhere.

Being formless, being everywhere and nowhere,
the Self has no motion and is not subject to passing time.
All things pass before the Self,
all things come to be witnessed,
What other reason can there be for the universe
than that it is to be witnessed?

If the mind falls still and contemplates,
it can admit and acknowledge the presence of the Self.
Such contemplation reveals that the Self,
being formless, limitless and unified,
is the same Self which hears through all ears,
sees through all eyes, witnesses through all senses,
as the Universal Witness.
In the physical world there are many bodies;
in the mental world there are many thoughts;
but that which witnesses all bodies and all thoughts
is the same Self, the One and Only I.
That Self is indivisible, all-pervading.
The Realisation of that Self reveals the Individual.

After many years, perhaps many lifetimes,
or believing one-self to be the body-image,
the Knowledge of the Self as being the Universal Witness
is a revelation of enormous significance.
It represents a great task of re-orientation or Education
since it runs contrary to the mass of belief held by humanity
where the body-image and its welfare are dominant.

In the Golden Age, the Individual Philosophy
is received by all men as undeniable
and is understood wholeheartedly. (*78*)
Knowing themselves to be the One Self,
there is no seeking to find identity in the eyes of others.
Knowing that in Reality no thing can be possessed,
there is no seeking to possess at the expense of others.
Knowing the natural law,
there is no seeking to alter or defy it.
Knowing the parts that have to be played,
there is the playing of those parts (*79*)
without fear as to how they may be judged.
Knowing that happiness does not depend on any thing,
there is no envy, jealousy, greed or hate.
Each resolving war in his own mind, resolves all war;
Each finding peace in his own mind, ensures all peace. (*80*)
But in the Iron Age,
the mind is blinded to the Self (*81*)
and each seeks to find in the Witnessed
what is already His as the Witness.

XVIII

Nothing

An essential, comforting and beautiful symbol,
representing an ultimate in human understanding
is Nought or Nothing. (*82*)
The mind requires that beyond which it is impossible to conceive,
a totality, an absolute;
and, as such, the idea of Nothing
is common and undeniable to all men.

Nothing is the only indivisible absolute
which the mind is capable of appreciating and understanding.
The only qualification of Nothing is that there is only One;
there cannot be two Nothings.
It cannot be multiplied nor subtracted from.
Nothing precedes and under-stands One.
One is created out of Nothing, standing simultaneously with it.
The unmanifest One is Nothing.
One can be divided, all numbers resulting from the division of One. (*83*)
One is continuously being divided and qualified,
depending always on Nothing to uphold it.
Nothing never changes, containing all that changes.
Nothing is the greatest mystery upon which the mind may dwell
and in which it finds its rest.

Nothing *must be appreciated positively;*
it is commonly appreciated negatively
as an unimportant absence of everything.

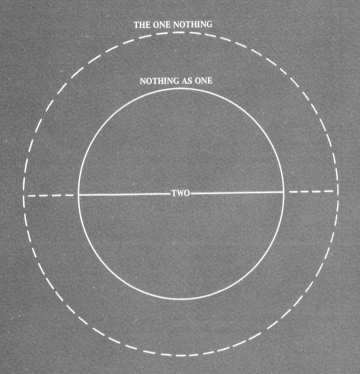

THE ONE NOTHING

NOTHING AS ONE

TWO

It is avoided by the ignorant because
dependent on identification with many things
for his own supposed identity,
an absence of everything is uncomfortable and unacceptable.

To be considered positively,
Nothing can be appreciated as the womb of All Things, (*84*)
the place of immaculate conception,
the never-changing background against which All Things come to pass.
"Nothing matters" can be the negative apathy of surrender by 'me'
or it can be the positive appreciation
of that which under-stands all that matters,
comes to matter, materialises.
It is Nothing that matters, makes matter.
As a sound depends on the ever-present silence
preceding it, containing it, subtending it, following it,
being always simultaneous with it,
so is Nought or Nothing to the One that is All Things. (*85*)
If there were no Nought, there could not be any thing
for there would not be anywhere for any thing to be,
in the same way that there could not be sound
without the silence in which to sound.
Nought is the place of the beginning, and the sustaining,
and the dissolving of All Things. (*86*)

The created Universe is One born of Nothing.
The One Nothing is 'before' and 'after' and 'without' the One. (*87*)
The apparent division, seeing or seeming two, of the One,
produces Two, the potential for creation being manifest — (*88*)
active-passive, positive-negative, energy-matter, light-dark,
male-female, man-womb of man, father-mother.
The Three, proceeding from the One as Two
is the Realisation by the One of Itself.

50

XIX *Perfection*

The Self witnesses the experience of all beings.
The Self has no form,
all forms being an expression or reflection of the Self.
All sensorily perceivable things are properties of the Self;
all mentally perceivable things are properties of the Self;
but the Self, being no thing, is
the One born of Nothing that contains All Things. (*89*)

The Self is de-ceived, robbed of birthright,
if the organ of discrimination in mind
believes any particular form to be the Self. (*90*)
If any thing is spoken of as 'i' or 'me' or 'mine', (*91*)
and believed in mind to be so,
the un-truth is spoken, the Self deluded.

There is only the One Self, which never changes,
and that Self witnesses the body and the contents of mind.
All the passing show of 'i's' and 'me's' are an illusion,
the cloud of assuming the Self to be that which it is not,
a cloud under which the mind labours
so long as there is for-getting and ignorance.
In Man is the miracle of a being able to contemplate its own existence
and it is only through the human being, amongst all forms of being,
that the Self may be re-membered.

So what, since the Self is no thing, can the Self be said to be?
When the question arises in the mind "Who am I?",

and it has become clear that in truth one is none of those things
that the Self has assumed Itself to be, what remains?

'I' may be considered as Consciousness, Knowledge, Bliss.
Pure Consciousness, pure Knowledge and pure Bliss
may be said to be the three aspects of the Self in Creation.
Before Creation, the Three are as One, the Same;
the Three in One are, in Creation, the One in Three.

In Creation,
the purest form of Consciousness is Knowing One Self to Be;
the purest form of Knowledge is Consciousness of Being the Self;
and Knowing the Consciousness of the Self
or Consciousness of Knowing the Self, is Bliss.
The Three in One is Truth; Truth expressed is One in Three.

Before Creation is caused, the three aspects of the Self,
pure Consciousness, pure Knowledge and pure Bliss,
remain in the formless, unmanifest, absolute potential
of the undeniable, ever-present Truth, Nothing.
In the beginning, the ever-present beginning, the eternal now,
the One Self, creating, becomes the three aspects,
and the potential becomes the dynamic expression, the Word.
The Self as Knowledge is expressed in form, according to the Word;
the Self as Consciousness is expressed as the Being of All Things;
and the Self as Bliss is the substance of All Things.
The Self, making All Things through Itself, makes Perfect;
and the Self, through the arising of Knowledge of Its own Being,
comes to Realise that Perfection through Man.
The Creation is not only than made Perfect
but, through Man, is seen to be Perfect.

I,
creating,
becomes,
in order to be,
I AM (*92*)

through Man,
I AM
becomes
KNOWING I AM,
the realisation of which is
BLISS.

In ignorance,
I AM
becomes
i am some thing,
and thinking being some thing
is the cause of un-happiness.

In truthfulness,
neither being nor becoming any thing, (*93*)
I AM NOTHING.
It is all just; just as it is. (*94*)

The Truth cannot be spoken since it is that which speaks.
The Truth cannot be described since it is before and beyond all description,
being that which describes all describable things.
The Truth, being the source of All Things,
all things are truthful at their level of expression.

XXI *Reality & Illusion*

The Self, creating,
carries all the creative force
of 'wanting to be something'.
As a consequence, 'wanting to be something'
is a powerful and natural force as man experiences it.
This outward-going creative force 'to be something'
leads away from, and obscures, its source which is nothing.
It is natural for the expressed being to desire to identify itself;
in looking for identity in its own creation
the Self naturally falls into ignorance,
ignoring and for-getting itSelf.

It is natural to come to believe
that the sensorily perceived world is the reality,
to give value to things, to identify with things,
to divide the universe into a multiplicity of separate things.
It requires Education to bring about disillusionment,
to be able to give the proper value,
the value appropriate, belonging, to things.
To remain in the belief in things themselves
is to remain within the limitations that such a belief imposes.
It is to put faith in the effect and deny the cause.
So committed to the effect does the mind become
that it is reluctant to admit the cause.
Confuse with the effect, refuse the cause.

When the mind is involved in the belief that
the sensorily perceived world is the reality,
value is given to things and they assume a positive existence. (*95*)
Hence, Nothing is considered negative
and a man who says he believes in nothing
means that he has found that he cannot believe in anything.
It is not surprising that he finds he cannot believe in anything.
A man who persists in believing in some thing
is de-ceiving the Self,
and sooner or later is bound to be disillusioned.
He is bound in order to be unbound.
There has to be the realisation that
He can only Believe, Be Free, in Nothing.

The mind *bound* to belief in the illusion is *bound* to be disillusioned
since all things alter, decay and die.
At birth, the mind is turned outwards to the senses and,
having come to believe in the reality of the sensorily perceived world,
disillusionment can be uncomfortable for,
without being aware of an alternative,
the mind clings tenaciously to familiar beliefs
and being parted from them is not easy.

Before a man can accept
that the only pure Believing is *in* Nothing,
he must give up belief in all things,
including vague concepts of 'god'. (*96*)
God as creator of All Things is Nothing.
Nothing is God. (*97*)
Believing in some-thing is the obverse of Believing *in* Nothing;
believing in some-thing is the refusal to Believe *in* God.

The positive Believing In the Substance Nothing is Belief *in* God.
Just Believe, Be-free, Be-loved.

The prelude to Wisdom is to realise that no thing is Known;
the beginning of Wisdom is to begin to Know Nothing. (*98*)
Man finds fulfilment in dis-covering Nothing,
that Nought out of which All Things appear
and into which All Things disappear.
That which appears out of Nothing is experience.

All Things that have been, are, and ever will be
are contained in the void and chaos of Nothing
where shines the light of the Self, pure Consciousness,
which, in any given moment now,
illuminates the forms of that moment,
revealing Knowledge of the Bliss of Perfect Creation.

God manifests, through Man, to HimSelf. (*99*)

'Mind' is a word carelessly used,
referred to often without consideration
by the speaker or writer as to what he means by it.
All attempts to define the word 'mind' in physical terms fail
and yet, when commonly used, it is assumed by the speaker,
writer, listener or reader that he knows what he means by it.
Mind is referred to and assumed to be
something related to, and yet something other than,
phenomena at the physical or sensory level of existence.
It is referred to and assumed to be
something that a man possesses.
Yet, where is it? What is it? How big is it?
Where does a man's mind begin and where does it end?

Observation and contemplation show
that mind cannot be described nor measured in physical terms.
Mind is thought to be somehow synonymous with brain.
Yet, where is what is heard, touched, seen, tasted, smelled?
Are the sounds translated by the aural mechanism
'inside' the brain or 'out there' in the world?
Do you see a star or an image in the mind called 'star'?
Is it not impossible to be sure whether what is sensed
is 'inside' the head or 'outside' it?
If a sensory experience is translated in the cortex of the brain,
how can it be known for sure what is 'out there'?
How can it be known with certainty
that one man's image of the world is the same as another's?

None of these questions can be answered satisfactorily
by the man who believes himself to be the body-image.
He who believes himself to have a separate and independent existence
believes himself to have a separate and independent mind,
and, believing in such an illusion,
he can never answer the problems of duality arising from such a view.

Only from the viewpoint of the One Self,
seeing objectively,
are such questions Known to be unanswerable
because, from that viewpoint,
there is no separate and independent entity
and therefore no duality,
and therefore no illusion of 'inside' and 'outside'.
It is essential not to confuse mind
with what the realms of mind contain.

When a man speaks of "having something *in* mind"
he speaks accurately.
He means that there is observation
of a thought or image *in* mind.

Observation and contemplation show
that the mind cannot be described
as a physical thing can be described.
All experiences are *in* mind,
are perceived *in* mind,
are contained *in* mind,
for where else could they be?

Science can never discover what mind *is*, as a describable phenomenon,
because the instruments of science are extensions of sensory
mechanisms
and are only capable of investigating phenomena
projected into the sensorily perceivable world.
Mind contains all science.
How could science investigate that which contains it?
Given that all things are experienced *in* mind,
the nearest that it is possible to approach an appreciation of mind
is to consider it space or void.

Mind is space
in the sense that all things are contained in space.
Mind is substantial, formless space —
'substantial' being that which 'stands under'
and 'formless' being that which has no shape and is therefore limitless.

Being limitless, there can only be one.
In truth, there is only One Mind
which contains all forms manifest —
'manifest' being that which is perceivable.
Everything is in Mind, for where else could it be?

It is not a question of experience being 'inside' or 'outside'.
The sensory experience of the world,
all experience in the mental realms,
they are all in the One Mind.
There is, in reality, no duality of
'in' and 'out', 'above' and 'below', 'before' and 'after';
these are all relative to the separate body-image in the physical world.

The belief in the world 'out there',
which is a projection of the belief in 'me' being 'here'.
is the illusion of duality.

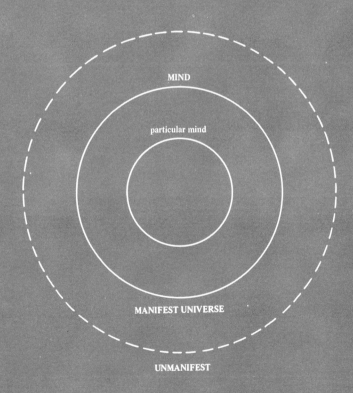

MIND

particular mind

MANIFEST UNIVERSE

UNMANIFEST

There is, in Reality,
only Experience Being Witnessed
by the One Self in the One Mind which has no defineable limits.

So what is meant by mind, 'my' mind?
What is being referred to is the particular organs of mind
associated with a particular being,
the processes of operation of those organs
and the particular forms being held or processed by those organs.
The organs of mind are the same in all human beings;
it is the forms of the contents that differ.
The belief in separate minds arises from the differing content
and the differing ways, according to experience,
that those contents are processed.

XXIII Contents of Mind

The experience of the sensorily perceived manifest world in Mind
might be called the Physical realm of Mind,
beyond which there is the 'darkness'
containing all unmanifest forms
incomprehensible to the organs of mind
because they are 'beyond' the consciousness of the Self
in any given moment.

There are two other realms of Mind
which have been given various names at different times
which we may call the Mental and Causal levels.

The Mental realm of Mind,
that which is ordinarily called mind,
is the realm containing the organs of mind —
the organs of thought and image processing —
and the thought and image forms themselves.

The Causal realm of Mind
causes everything to appear as it does.
Ideas from the unmanifest region of the Causal realm
manifest in the 'light' of Consciousness, the Self.
The ideas about the Self
cause all things to appear in the mind as they do.

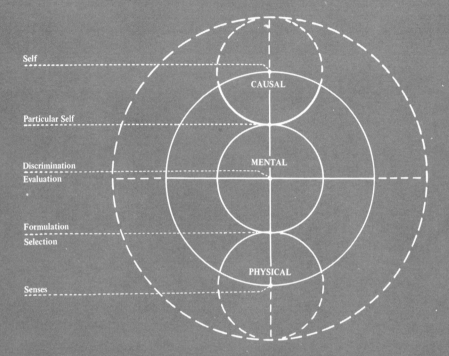

Self

Particular Self

Discrimination
Evaluation

CAUSAL

MENTAL

Formulation
Selection

PHYSICAL

Senses

64

The two principal organs of mind are
the organ of evaluation/discrimination
and the organ of selection/formulation.

The organ of selection-formulation
selects sensory images and formulates thoughts. (*100*)
The organ of evaluation-discrimination
evaluates and decides,
giving or refusing assent,
accepting or rejecting what is formulated.

When the particular beliefs in mind are dissolved,
particular mind loses its limitations and expands into One Mind. (*101*)

The organ of evaluation-discrimination,
at the centre of particular mind,
serves desire.
It is the same organ of mind at the centre of One Mind
where it serves need,
discriminating between self-ish and self-less.
Need is 'outside' particular mind; desire 'in' it.
Being at the centre of Mind, the discriminator is crucial,
the Cross that all men bear. (*102*)

XXIV Realisation

Before the beginning of Creation,
the One Self,
Self-contained, Self-content, Self-dependent, Self-conscious,
is Nothing.
In the act of Creation,
when the Word is spoken,
the Self, needing to be Known to itSelf, to be Something,
manifests to itSelf, creating the apparent space of Mind.
All Things are in One Mind.
All Things being 'made-through' the Self are Per-fect,
coming to pass inexorably, being under the law of the Word.
All Things are a reflection of the Self.
The Self observes, 'projects in front of itself',
and reflects upon its own reflection,
as in a mirror,
creating in order to Know its own Being. (*103*)

Through creating,
the Self identifies with itself.
The Self in projecting itself forgets,
taking its manifested reflection for itself,
'falling in love with its own reflection', (*104*)
the Creator appearing to become its own Creation,
as a man may look in a mirror and say "That's me".
By the directing of the organ of discrimination towards the senses,
the reflection is taken for the real.

The work of Education in man is the freeing of the organ
of evaluation-discrimination from false belief and identity
so that it admits remembrance of the Self.
The Self is re-instated as the Reality
by the dissolution of the fictitious, supposedly separate,
illusory self called 'me'.

The human is the one being in form
with an organ of discrimination which can realise, make real,
the Self by ceasing to create the illusion of a separate self.
In re-membering the Self, the human being becomes Man.
The Self, through the form Man,
disengages itself from involvement (*105*)
in its own Creation, working through the organ of discrimination
with the power of Reason, (*106*)
'the sound of things'.

The human being,
being made in the image of the Self,
reflects the process.
Born into ignorance, the evaluator attempts to find identity.
Needing to find identity,
the evaluator establishes the particular body-image as the self.
Desiring then to furnish it with a particular, outstanding identity,
one that will differentiate that particular being from all others,
there follows the claiming of particular properties
and characteristics as 'mine'.
Having lost true identity,
the human being can spend a lifetime
creating a fictional identity,
this desire manifesting as wanting to be recognised as 'somebody'.

By proving through acclaim or notoriety
that he really does exist as a separate entity,
by being recognised by others as being 'somebody',
he can persuade himself that he exists and knows who he is.

Because he attains power, wealth, fame, success and so on,
in worldly terms he stands marked above the insignificant.
All this is vanity, emptiness, and Self-deception, (*107*)
continually robbing the Self of its re-birth,
its disengagement from the reflection of itself
so that it may witness the Perfection.

True and lasting identity
can never be found among the things of the world;
all such fabrications turn to dust.
Only the human being,
as distinct from all other beings from stones to monkeys,
may, through the organ of discrimination, be freed
from false identification
and evolve to re-member the Self,
make the Self Real or Royal.

All Things are unrealised beings;
only Man can realise that Being.
Achieving Manhood,
Man witnesses the Creation as the reflection of Himself,
the Self being resurrected in Man. (*108*)

XXV Mattering

Id-entification means to make an entity out of the id, 'that'.
Identification means to make an entity out of the form
made manifest by Consciousness, the Self.
The principle organ of the mind
is the organ of evaluation-discrimination
the organ which gives value and meaning,
and, according to that evaluation, discriminates,
apparently choosing between one and another.
The Education of this organ of mind
is the essence of the preparatory work
that reveals the Individual Philosophy —
what value to give to experience presented in any given moment,
to discriminate between the Real and the illusion,
between Self and non-Self. (*109*)

Forms themselves are neutral. (*110*)
As a passing show, they present themselves in the present.
They grow, change, decay and pass.
The Self, disengaged, simply witnesses the passing show, (*111*)
the reflection of Itself.
It is the organ of evaluation-discrimination that gives value,
in ignorance according to belief,
in Truth according to Knowledge,
as the forms manifest in the light of Self-Consciousness,
appearing out of the unmanifest,
the mater, matrix, Mother Earth,
obeying the Word, the Law, the Lord, the Father in Heaven.

The art of the evaluator 'within' creation
is to give appropriate value,
to give proper weight to matters.
Things matter only to the degree that the evaluator-discriminator
allows them to matter.
The more weight they are given,
the more they matter.
The denser they become, the more the mind is loaded
and the greater the amount of Self-Consciousness, Being, they absorb.

The situation presented in any given moment is neutral.
The *import*ance attached to it is *import*ed.
When the heart is heavy and the spirit depressed,
when there is great weight on the mind,
it is because importance has been ascribed and permitted.
And this is in contrast to the state of happiness
when the heart is light and the spirit free.

Due to the 'outward' thrust of creation,
the tendency of the uneducated discriminator,
surrounded by false belief,
is to permit weight, analagous to gravity.
The more *grave* the situation is permitted to become,
the closer the being comes to the *grave*,
the absence of consciousness,
the point where Self-Consciousness is completely absorbed.
So sunk in thoughts and imaginings does the mind become that,
when the mind clears again,
it is as if the Self had not been aware of Itself existing.

The evaluator-discriminator only evaluates and discriminates
appropriately and accurately
in the light of the Self, Consciousness,
in obedience to the Self, Knowledge, (*112*)
arising out of the situation, meeting the needs of the situation; (*113*)
never when bound by false belief
and interfered with by the illusion of 'me' and 'mine'.
Surrounded by false belief,
the evaluator-discriminator works for the benefit
of an illusory and fictitious non-entity,
concerns itself with 'my' comfort, 'my' rights, 'my' survival,
and the maintenance of 'my' image.
When you are dead, who cares about your hopes and fears,
your failures and successes, your ambitions and achievements?
They may remember your deeds, but do they remember you?

How does 'me' arise?
An object exists in its own right and is observed.
As soon as some concept, belief, assumption, attitude, opinion
in relation to that object arises in the mind,
'me' is created,
as the supposedly separate one who holds that belief
about that object.
The trouble starts when 'me' then makes some requirement
upon that object for 'my' benefit.

In creation, things appear to matter, become matter;
In Truth, it is Nothing that matters
and no thing is permitted to matter.

The Self as expression or creation
is Absolute as One in Three,
the Three being as One, the Three aspects of One;
being the Witness of Creation, Consciousness;
being the Experience of Creation, Knowledge;
and being the Substance of Creation, Bliss.
The Absolute as One in Three is eternal, 'within' time;
The Absolute as the One Nothing is everlasting, 'beyond' time,
being ever-present 'before' creation
and yet being simultaneous with it,
in the same way that sound depends on the ever-present silence
preceding it, containing it and following it,
silence being simultaneous with the sound.
The vibrating substance of silence being sound,
the shape of the sound is impressed in silence,
as clay when formed into a pot remains clay.
If there were no substance of silence, there would be no sound;
If there were not the Bliss of Nothing, there would not be anything.

As sound depends on silence for its expression,
so the expression of the One Self, Creation,
depends on the ever-present pre-Creation state,
the state of the Nought or the One Nothing.
Though silence does not have manifestly perceivable properties,
the presence of silence is experienced as the absence of sound;
Similarly,
the eternal Self is comprehended in the absence of the non-Self.

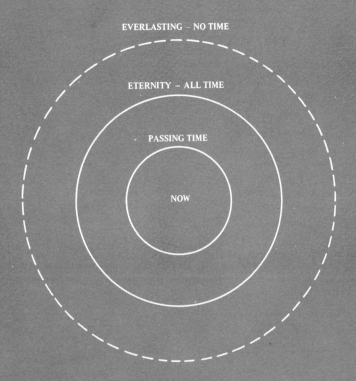

This means that, in order that the Self may be discovered,
the mind must become free of all the beliefs in 'me'
and the Mind must become free of all the ideas *about* the Self.
In order to be realised,
the Self must be free of what it is not.

Commonly when the word 'mind' is used
what is referred to is the contents of mind.
Once the Self, through identification, has fallen into ignorance
and the organ of discrimination has become surrounded
by a cloud of beliefs,
and has existed many years under the shadow and dominion
of that bondage,
it is not easy for those bonds to be loosened.
Upon the constancy of the belief that the man is his body-image
hangs his view of the world,
including the assumption
that the sensorily perceived world is the world of permanence,
the world of reality upon which he can depend and put his trust,
that which is royal and worthy of worship.
This view carries a host of other beliefs and assumptions.
For example, he takes the view that he is a small, substantial entity
surrounded by a universe so large that its size
is impossible to comprehend.
To him — or rather, to his evaluator —
the body — and therefore 'he' — has a size and limit
and the universe expands to an indefinite edge.
He believes in physical years of passing time,
believes he is born, lives and dies in that time.

His view, concentrated on this period of one physical embodiment,
is that the life of the universe
stretches backwards and forwards beyond his comprehension
to an infinite measurement in both directions.
He cannot satisfactorily conceive of a starting point (*114*)
and an end point of the universe.
He assumes himself to have a spontaneous birth
and a cataclysmic death,
though often persuading himself that 'he' continues after death.
'Infinity' is his vague way out of the dilemma,
using it to cover up an open-ended existence,
so that he can stand unsteadily, blinkered,
on his little island of arbitrary physical measurement
explaining away the incomprehensible as irrelevant to 'his' life.

Yet how different are the possibilities
when the belief in the body-image as the Self is dissolved.
Supposing the view of himself as a small physical entity
surrounded by a vast physical universe is supplanted
and it is realised that all experience is in Mind
and that Mind contains the Universe as He alone sees it?
Age and size, time and space are then no longer relevant.
There are no finite measurements in Mind;
there is no believing in limits.
The infinite, the undefined, come to have real meaning
and there is Knowing that limits are a super-imposition.
With no limits super-imposed,
mind becomes Mind.

The beginning and ending of Himself are then meaningless.
The beginning is an eternal beginning
and the end an eternal ending. (*115*)
In the *present*, the *present* or gift of now,
is the *Presence* or Being of now, the *pre-sense* state.
He becomes again as a baby, unified,
yet, whereas then he was innocent, unknowing,
now He Knows He Is.

As an example, an analogy, of this liberating of the mind,
where the bondage of duality is transcended
and the unity of Mind revealed,
consider the sun in relation to the earth.
The mind committed to the view of the body-image,
the earth-bound view,
thinks of the sunrise followed by the sunset followed
by the sunrise and so on;
yet, from the detached, unified view, it is comprehended that,
as the earth turns,
somewhere there is always sunrise and somewhere always sunset.
There is always sunrise and sunset co-existing.
Eternity is thought of, from the body-image point of view,
as a continuous repetition on the line of passing time:
from the point of view of the Self,
eternity is the co-existence of everything now,
and it is seen that not only do sunrise and sunset co-exist
but that their rising and setting is an illusion
for, in reality, the sun never rises nor sets;
it is always shining.

XXVII *Goodness*

The evaluating and discriminating organ of mind,
having become *used* to being turned
to the Physical or sensorily perceived realm of Mind,
and being used to the laws and interpretations at that level,
always has a tendency to want to measure and locate in those terms.
Hence the tendency to want to locate the Self —
to want to think of it as being above or in front of or within,
that is to say, at a distance from that which is witnessed.
It is the habitual working of the evaluator
because ordinarily it works dualistically
through contrast and comparison.
As intellect it tends to create duality, separation and multiplicity
and it is not easy therefore
for the mind to admit the unity of the Self,
to appreciate that the Witness, and the Witnessed
and the act of Witnessing are the same,
the three aspects of the Self that are inseparably one.
The Self does not have location in relation to something else
because it *is* everything.
The Witness and the Witnessed are not separate
any more than the clay and the pot are separate.

Another example of the change from the dual to the unified view
is to consider energy and matter.
From the scientific or physical point of view
energy and matter are two different phenomena,
although from time to time they are thought of as interchangeable.

From the level of sensory perception,
it is understandable that they are thought of dualistically
because the two names are used to describe two states,
one finer and one denser in relation to some arbitrary mid-point.

As an analogy, consider 'soft' and 'hard';
this duality describes to the tactile sense
things that are soft and things that are hard
in relationship to an arbitrary yardstick, say the human body.
In the unified view, there cannot be soft *and* hard;
there can be degrees of softness *or* degrees of hardness;
two evaluations are not necessary
because either softness is a degree of hardness
or hardness is a degree of softness.

So, concerning energy and matter, it is possible to comprehend that
from a superlatively fine point, the Self,
the whole spectrum of phenomena would be seen as
either all energy *or* all matter,
in differing degrees of concentration but all unified.
From the superlatively fine and ultimate point, the Self,
energy is matter *or* matter is energy.

Further, then, there can only be the duality of good and evil-bad
as long as there is something in relation to which
there can be a bettering or worsening of condition.
Hence, in relation to the body, the Physical realm of Mind,
there can be that which is good or evil-bad for the body;
and, in relation to the Mental realm of Mind,
there can be that which is good or evil-bad to think.

Good, in this context, may be defined as that which promotes
well-being, equilibrium, equanimity,
in contrast with evil-bad as that which promotes
illness, disturbance, tension, conflict.

At these two levels, physical and mental,
good and evil-bad are valid and useful as words
to describe a bettering or worsening of condition;
but, in Reality, from the superlative view of the Self,
there is no good *and* evil-bad (*116*)
in the sense of two factions opposed to each other.

To illustrate this, visualise a point source
which we may call Good or God.
From this point, draw a line, the drawing outwards of the line
from source representing the 'outward' thrust of creation
and the line itself as the Creation.
The line Creation, issueing from the source point Good,
is all Good, being Good, of God.
Now, any point moving along that line has two directions
in which to move, either towards the source or away from it.
As far as the moving point is concerned, any movement
towards the source is towards Good and is a bettering,
whilst any movement away from the source is,
in contrast to the other movement, away from Good.
To describe the movement away from source
it is convenient to introduce another word
and that moving away, that worsening of condition, is called evil-bad.
Any movement away from the omnipotent, motionless Good
must be a worsening and, therefore, evil-bad,
and there must be a worsening before there can be a bettering.

So, from the finest viewpoint, the Self, the One that is motionless,
all Creation, which is ever in motion, is all Good, all God.
All is as it must be, Perfect.
But, from any viewpoint within that Creation,
there is always in the constant motion
a moving towards Good and a moving away,
movement conducive to Self-Realisation and movement unfavourable.
Evil-bad has to be invented as a concept
to describe the changing, relative degrees of Goodness.
There is, in Reality, only Good or God,
but, in Creation, in motion, there are degrees of goodness.
The Self observes that everything is Good,
which is to see that everything is Just, just as it should be.
That which is in Creation suffers;
that which witnesses Creation suffers to be.
All things suffer in order to be.

That which men call evil is that which blinds them, or appears
to move them away from the realisation that all is Good or God.
When it is seen that all is Good, *there is no evil.* (*117*)
Whilst it is believed that there is evil,
that which appears to be opposed to Good, then there is evil. (*118*)

From the still source, the Self in every man,
all is Good, God-made, Perfect; (*119*)
and the devil and all his works are inventions to describe
those influences which move the viewpoint away from that realisation.
It is the devil's influence that causes men to believe
that there are both Good *and* evil. (*120*)
But there cannot be two; evil is a degree of goodness, (*121*)
and is necessary for the Realisation of Goodness, God.

The devil is depicted as the tempter to sensory pleasure
and in the sense that man when born is drawn to the senses
and comes to believe in the reality of the sensorily perceived
world and fulfilment therein,
then he may be said to have been tempted and fallen.
And in the sense that he may continue in this belief,
continuing pursuit of fulfilment in that direction,
ignoring the Self as the source and the fulfilment,
then he may be said to worship the devil,
and he will suffer all the disappointments, bewilderment and fear
that such a direction inexorably brings.
Failing to realise that all his sufferings
are due to his own ignorance,
he invents the devil and evil as being *apart* from himself,
not realising that they are *a part* of Himself.

Since the uneducated discriminator is *used* to duality
and permits belief in factions being in opposition to each other,
there is set up this tendency to equate evil-bad with Good,
believing them to be two opposing factions.
Evil is not opposed to Good (*122*)
any more than darkness is opposed to light.
They are not opposites
but degrees of absence or presence.
Inasmuch as darkness may be said to be an absence of light —
no one says that light is an absence of darkness —
so evil may be said to be an absence of Good.
But there is never an absence of Good
any more than the sun ceases to shine.

It is a case of how far from the source point Good
or how weak or obscured the light.
From the light's point of view, there is no such thing as darkness;
it is only when moving away from or obscuring the light
that the power of light decreases or darkness increases.

Because the subtleness of the unified view is at first elusive,
many teachers and religions have fallen for the dualistic view
and have placed evil as equal and opposite to Good.
It is an understandable but mis-leading trap.
It is like saying that the positive and negative wires
in an electric current are in opposition;
there have to be both for there to be light.
Or it is like saying that cleanliness is opposed to dirtiness;
remove the dirt and the cleanliness is there;
it is not possible to put in cleanliness, only to remove the dirt. (*123*)
Likewise for the created being,
evil is essential to the realisation of God
and it often transpires that that which men call evil
from the body-image view of the world
is beneficial in terms of spiritual evolution.

It is often suggested in religious writings and teachings
that sensory pleasure is to be shunned as the work of the devil
because it is in opposition to service to God
and this causes an apparent dichotomy,
dividing that which is Good or God
from that which is Good-made or God-made.
The creation of this duality might appropriately be called
the devil's work in that it divides instead of unifies,
causing much stress and disturbance of mind.

The key to this mistake is its limited context.
It could be said that
the blind *pursuit* of sensory pleasure is evil,
if that pleasure is sought in the belief that it is itself
the source of lasting happiness and fulfilment:
for then there is the ignoring of the real source,
the blinding of the mind to God.
But, in itself, not for itself alone,
sensory pleasure is Good, God-made, made to be enjoyed. (*124*)
It is the excessive pursuit in ignorance, (*125*)
as distinct from grateful acceptance in moderation, (*126*)
that misleads and confuses the discriminator.

As the Self, Consciousness, becomes involved in the Creation,
so, according to the degree to which things come to matter,
energy appears to decrease *or* matter to increase.
The Self, becoming in-volved, 'turns into' the Creation,
making things matter through identification.
The more intense, in-tense, the involvement,
the less the consciousness *or* the denser the substance.
From the superlatively fine point of the Self,
any involvement is an illusion, 'in the play',
in that the Self appears to be involved in the play of forms,
the per-form-ance. (*127*)
The more involved the Self becomes,
the more deceived, de-ceived, the Self.

Hence, man's evolution lies not in becoming something
that he is not already,
but in e-volving the Self, turning the Self out from,
to become the Witness instead of being in-volved at any level. (*128*)

An indication of the failure to evolve
is the example of the man entering senility
who becomes more and more 'turned in'
until he is only concerned with the comfort of the body,
his mind living increasingly on a diet of stale memories
until he is barely conscious of anything other than his imaginings.
Beyond that,
there is only the falling back into the unconsciousness called death.

That which can be taken away is not You;
that which cannot be taken away is You;
and that which cannot be taken away from You is You. (*129*)

When the first state, the finest state,
pure Consciousness, pure Knowledge, pure Bliss,
is moved from the state of potential to a state of expression,
there is a change from a state of static equilibrium
to one of moving equilibrium, the Universe or Creation. (*13*)
The moving equilibrium is threefold,
these three movements being called for example
creating, maintaining, dissolving.
Man's part in the Universe, his responsibility as a particular being,
is the work assigned to him
in the creating, maintaining and dissolving process.
That part is 'written'
and there is nothing he can do to change it.
But, in coming to play the part, (*130*)
there is forgetting that it is only a part (*131*)
in the moving equilibrium of the Universe,
and the original state of static equilibrium is forgotten.
In ignorance, identified with the body-image,
there is a seeking to find the static or constant in the moving, (*132*)
a task impossible to fulfil.
Hence, the desire to find the static or the constant in Creation,
which is experienced as lack of equanimity in mind,
is a looking in the wrong direction to fulfil man's higher purpose,
Self-Realisation, realisation of the constant equilibrium
that is Nothing, God.

This search finds expression in the moving equilibrium as
the desire for happiness — pleasure and comfort for 'me',
the desire for knowledge — learning for 'my' benefit,
and the desire for immortality — seeking 'my' identity
and evidence of 'my' survival after death.
These are but the shadows of
pure Bliss, pure Knowledge, pure Consciousness. (*133*)
The desire for happiness, knowledge and immortality for 'me'
leads to excessive behaviour, be-having,
the pursuit regardless of others
which begets unhappiness, ignorance and death.

Bliss and happiness might be distinguished here;
happiness can be described as a state of well-being
in relation to things,
as when "all's well with the world".
But it does not last since circumstances inexorably change.
Bliss, however, is a state of well-being independent of things
and people are sometimes described as being in such a state
when, to all outward appearances and by conventional standards,
their situation would appear to be far from satisfactory.
Thus, happiness belongs to the world
whilst Bliss is "out of this world". (*134*)

All men's actions, selfish actions,
are motivated basically by three desires,
the desire for happiness, for knowledge, for immortality.
Sometimes the connection is obvious, sometimes not so easy to see,
especially when they appear as their reverse
in minds that are perverted, 'turned through' to the negative.

Pure Consciousness, pure Knowledge and pure Bliss,
which are as One in Nothing,
is the equilibrium of full Self-Realisation,
the equilibrium 'beyond' Creation, attained through resurrection,
the death of the fictional self that raises the real Self.
Its complement or reverse
is experienced as the 'gravitational' pull towards inertia,
towards absence of Self-Consciousness, unconsciousness,
the equilibrium of the 'darkness' of sleep and death. (*135*)
Both death and Self-Realisation are states of refuge and rest.
The reverse of attaining Self-Realisation is suicide.

The potential state, static equilibrium,
as energy motionless or unexpressed,
may be said to be the male or 'sire' state of the Self:
And the potential state, static equilibrium,
as matter motionless or unmoved,
may be said to be the female or matter-mother state of the Self.
The two states are two aspects of the same,
the female being projected or taken out of the male, (*136*)
the de-siring of the male.
The apparent inter-action of the two,
an illusion since they are really one, (*137*)
is procreative,
before or on be*half* of Creation
producing the illusory Creation.

Knowledge of Being, I AM, the purest state of the Self in Creation,(*138*)
moves, under the power of desire, to wanting to be some-thing,
which leads to identification when a name is given to some thing
and it is believed to be that thing as a separate entity. (*139*)
When meaning is given to a situation,
and the discriminator accepts that meaning as truth,
the Being becomes involved,
the force of consciousness going into that situation
giving it importance and existence manifest
so that Consciousness of Being is lost
and it is as if the thing or the situation only exists.
The Being becomes unconscious of Itself.
It is in this respect that some thing possesses the Being. (*140*)
Hence, when a man says he has possessions and believes it,
it is meant that there is identification with certain objects
which, in Reality, possess Him.
And so, when exhorted to give up possessions,
what is meant is the cessation of identification with objects
which have hitherto had the power to possess the Being.
The demons which are said to possess a man
are the beliefs and assumptions in mind which have the power
to 'steal' the Knowledge of the Self.
The power of the Educated discriminator is such that
it may cast out these demons with the undeniable Knowledge I AM.
People, believing it is they who possess, say they have belongings;
belongings, be-longings, are *longings-to-be*;
the Self *is* when there are no more belongings.

XXX   *Attention*

The Self expressed in each Being is the state I AM; (*141*)
Man, amongst all creatures, being raised above all creatures, may
KNOW I AM,
a Knowledge that arises through the Self observing the Creation
and realising it to be a reflection of Itself.
This Knowing I AM is experienced in the passive state of mind.
In the active state of mind, desires involve the Self,
and Consciousness of Being
becomes Consciousness of something separate from the Self.
Being conscious of some thing in particular
is the selecting or separating off of a form or assembly of forms.
The line of connection between apparent subject and object
is a line of witnessing or consciousness called attention, (*142*)
which means 'a stretching or holding before'.
It is then a matter of belief, belief making matter,
which is to say, the degree of identification with the object,
the degree to which it is permitted — sent through — to become real
at the expense of — hang or weigh from — consciousness of Being;
'-pense', in Latin, meaning hang or weigh, is a verb used to
indicate measuring both heaviness and value.
Consciousness of Being expends itself
in giving weight or value to some thing.
If a man says "I believe that"
he means that he leases his Being to it, so that it is.

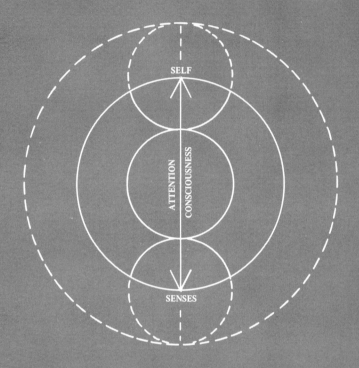

Is attention given or taken?
If given, to what and why? If taken, by what and why?
Who or what gives attention and why?

The Self, as Consciousness, is the source of attention
and for attention to be given to something, that thing must take it,
the giving and the taking being simultaneous.
Attention is given-taken in response to need or desire,
desire being subjective and need being objective.
Attention is held between the Self and some thing
and the medium through which the attention passes is the mind.
The selector-formulator organ of mind
receives a continuous flood of sensory impressions and mental forms,
except in deep sleep and death,
selecting that which is significant
either in relation to desires if desires are active or stimulated
or in relation to that which is significant in itself,
that which is needing attention.

In the state of mind disturbed by desires for 'me'
attraction to some thing gives rise to tension, (*143*)
the striving for 'me' and 'mine',
the looking for that which will satisfy 'my' desires — subjective.
In the state of mind undisturbed by desires,
there is attraction to that which is needful
without tension — objective.
The disturbed state of mind is inquisitive, acquisitive;
the undisturbed state, being of One Mind, is accepting, receptive.

It is in these two conditions of attention given-taken
that the organ of evaluation-discrimination plays its part
to decide whether attention is appropriate or not, (144)
whether to continue to give attention or to withdraw it.
In the disturbed state,
when the discriminator is uneducated and confused with belief,
it has little or no power over attention
and attention is permitted indiscriminately
in response to any stimulus related to any desire.
In the undisturbed state,
when the discriminator is educated and receptive to Knowledge,
it has the power to withdraw attention, (145)
distinguishing between healthy, appropriate occupation
and harmful, useless indulgence.
Bringing the mind to the undisturbed state, being of One Mind,
attention is given to that which needs it, for as long as it needs it.

In the state of mind undisturbed by 'me' and 'my' requirements,
the Self, observing Itself, meets the needs of Creation, (146)
the attention being given naturally to that which needs it.
The three great desires of the mind gradually become satisfied,
since all things inform of the Self, Knowledge,
all things are seen to be Perfect, Bliss,
and the Consciousness of Being, which is perfect freedom,
eliminates misconception concerning death. (147)
In the disturbed state of mind,
in the presence of false beliefs and the desires powered by those beliefs,
there is the excessive and often inappropriate pursuit of happiness
in the form of possessions, pleasure and comfort,
there is the excessive and often inappropriate pursuit of knowledge
in the form of learning about useless things,
and the excessive and often inappropriate pursuit of immortality

in the form of excessive concern for the health of the body
and the useless search for evidence of 'my' after-life.

Once attention is given-taken, there are two possibilities,
dependent on the power of the discriminator.
If the discriminator is weak, involvement will be automatic
and will be such that the object will absorb consciousness
so that Consciousness of Being is lost.
Without control over loss of Being,
it is as if the man is continually asleep,
rarely aware of Himself as the organs of mind are pulled
hither and thither by succeeding desires and imaginings.
If the discriminator is strong, involvement will be controlled.
Either attention will be withdrawn
if the continuation of attention seems inappropriate;
or attention will be permitted to continue
to meet the need of the situation.
When the need has been met, attention is withdrawn
and the restful state of Consciousness of Being retrieved.
This is the service that is perfect freedom
because there is no frustrating bondage
of 'me' requiring a result for 'myself'.

In the undisturbed state, when attention rests,
as, for example, on natural beauty,
the mind is filled with awe, wonder, humility, gratitude —
humility being related to humus, human, "being brought to earth",
and gratitude to that which is freely given.

Apart from attention being given to the sensorily perceived world,
there is attention given to the processes of the mental world,
the parade of word forms and structures and the picture images.
The permitting of existence to this mental parade
is what is commonly called thinking.

'Thinking' is a word so indiscriminately used
that it has lost precise meaning.
It is commonly used to describe any process in the mental realm,
frequently being used and confused with such words as:
formulating, visualising, considering, contemplating,
reasoning, imagining, dreaming, and so on.

After formulating — putting into word form,
and visualising — putting into picture images,
both prerequisites of all mind processes,
the first and most important distinction between the above words
is between those that apply to the mental realm
in the undisturbed state, at One with Mind,
and those that apply to the mental realm
in the disturbed state, when apparently separate and particular.

For the mental realm in the undisturbed state,
considering — 'with the stars',
contemplating — 'with the template' or 'temple' or 'open space'
and reasoning — 'the sound of things'
are appropriate.

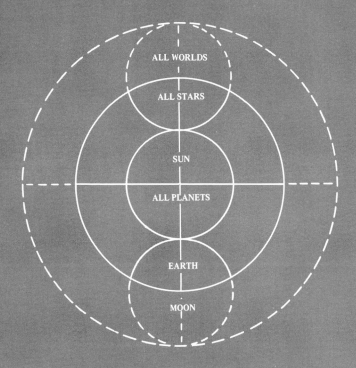

In considering, contemplating and reasoning,
there is objectivity — no desire or concern for 'me'.
The mind is still and receptive,
allowing a flowing through, a coming to pass.
Beliefs do not interfere, make-between,
and do not cause the super-imposition of 'my' requirements
on what is there of its own accord,
thus allowing the harmonious revelation of what is to be revealed.
It is a disposition to admit,
the permitting, sending through, of inspiration, breathing into.

For the mental realm in the disturbed state,
the words thinking, imagining and day-dreaming are appropriate,
and here there is a distinction between directed and undirected
processes.
Directed processes are those motivated by the desire
for a particular result for 'me' and might collectively be called
'thinking *about*' the situation.
This thinking is sometimes called "circling thought"
and it includes categories of imagining —
the projection of past situations irrelevant to the present
and of imaginary future situations as in 'wishful' thinking.
Imagining is distinct from visualising
which is concerned with an actual situation.
These directed or intentional, intent-intense, processes
are usually motivated by the desire to gain or avoid something, *(148)*
and they are usually associated with feelings or emotions such as:
fear, hatred, anger, excitement, envy, lust, greed —
all expenditures of energy that are succeeded by:
apathy, inertia, laziness, sadness, depression,
all indications of energy dissipated. *(149)*

Such inappropriate processes, deleterious to the organism,
tend to cloud awareness of the present moment.
When thinking and imagining, the Consciousness of Being
is forsaken, surrendered for the sake of the mental parade.
The force of consciousness is absorbed to a greater or lesser degree,
dimming perception of the sensorily perceived world — absent-minded.
It is impossible to think
and be fully aware of sensory images at the same time; (*150*)
nor is it possible to be thinking and be Conscious of Being.
It is not possible to think *and* be.
These subjective processes are obstructive
as distinct from considering, contemplating and reasoning
which are objective and constructive,
being carried out to meet the need of the present moment.
It is only though observation of these two ways of working
that the evaluator-discriminator, aided by Conscience,
is able to desist from the idle, the useless and the destructive. (*151*)

The undirected processes of thinking
are those random sequences of images called day-dreaming.
They are not motivated by the desire for a particular result
though they are powered by desires and fears based on false belief.
They are all useless and cut out Consciousness of Being;
they are detri-mental, 'rubbing-down-the-mind'.

When thinking, imagining and dreaming,
the mind is closed, involved and in flux.
When considering, contemplating and reasoning,
the mind is open and still, being of One Mind.
When not working, remaining Conscious of Being,
the mind is in a state of meditation. (*152*)

Memory is the essential background to mental processes
and it is useful to distinguish between Mental and Causal memory.
Mental memory is that which records the experience and learning
received during the current physical embodiment.
Thinking, imagining and dreaming are all based on past experience
and learning related to 'this life'.
Causal memory is that of Conscience (*153*)
and it is the source of that Knowing which has not been taught
and has thus not been learned during the current embodiment.
It arises out of the present and is appreciated in the present,
being revealed when considering, contemplating and reasoning.

For example, reason being 'the sound of things',
a man may say "That *sounds* reasonable".
If this expression is being used correctly,
the user will observe that he is relying on
a sense of judgment, rightness, righteousness,
that he has never had to be taught.
It may even be in conflict with what he has been taught to believe.
Further, if something in these writings is recognised as valid,
something that has not been encountered before,
it is re-cognised, re-Known,
because it is already there and responding in Causal memory.
The Bible does not contain the Truth;
its value lies in its ability to illuminate
what is already Known in memory. (*154*)
Otherwise, how could it be judged that what the Bible says is right?

The seat of memory is often described as the heart, (*155*)
"He knew in his heart",
and it is distinct from the remembered learning of the head.

The sound of Reason
is the 'voice' of Conscience, In-Tuition, (*156*)
and it is the memory of an innate Knowledge working,
a memory that is the same in all human beings
though covered to differing degrees in particular minds.
Being common Knowledge,
it is expressed as common sense,
as, for example, with the common sense of decency,
that which is fitting.

Through contemplation and considering, reason works,
revealing the Knowledge required
both to Realise the Real and to meet need.
The revelation is presented as a present in the present.
It is given in response to the situation
and, in meeting that situation conscientiously,
each receives what he needs to Know precisely, pre-cut.
The situation is tailored exactly for the requirements of that mind.
This must be so since the Self is witnessing Itself.
The Knowledge is always there before the cloud of imaginings
about 'me' and 'my' supposed relationship with the situation
descend quickly upon it,
before the super-imposed thinking and imagining
as to how the situation affects the fictional 'me' and 'mine'.

XXXIII   *One, Two, Three*

There is only One.
Two must arise from One
because Two is the concept of Two Ones.

Two and One cannot exist together as both real;
for if there is One, there cannot be Two,
and, if there are Two, there cannot be One.

If One is real, Two are an illusion;
If Two are real, One is an illusion;
but, since Two arises from One,
One must be the Reality and Two the illusion.

There is only One.
Given the Reality that there is only One,
Two, as One plus One or Two halves of One, must be an illusion.
If there is One, there cannot be another One;
therefore, One plus One is an impossibility;
therefore, the illusory Two must be Two halves of One.
One is as it really *is*
but, in creation, the One appears to divide
and there appear to be Two —
witness and witnessed, subject and object, here and there,
and so on.
Out of the apparent division into Two
there arises the possibility of the realisation that there is only One.
The Real is One, Two is an illusion, Three is Realisation of the One.

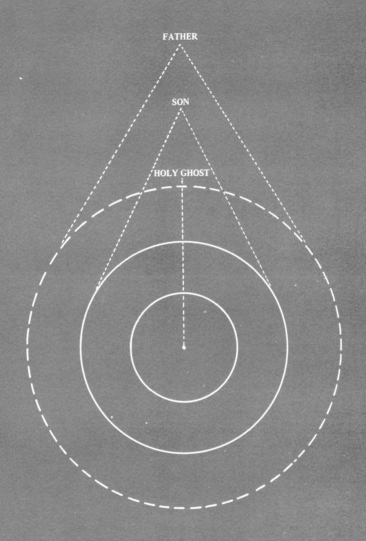

FATHER

SON

HOLY GHOST

The One Nothing is the Father,
the Same; (*157*)

The Nothing as One is the Son, the Second,
the Same; (*158*)

And the Third, the Realising of the One, is the Holy Ghost, (*159*)
the Spirit of Knowledge,
arising from the Father and the Son.

Desiring is due, in Creation, to apparent separation
instability and incompleteness.
That which appears to lack is moved to complete itself
and the power that draws to completeness is called Love. (*160*)
The desire to complete, to unify,
is to feel the unifying power of the Reality of One, (*161*)
in contrast with the intolerable discomfort of Two, duality.
The universal, unifying principle of Love (*162*)
is that which holds the Universe as One,
and that which causes apparent separation
is the divisive or destructive principle, Two.
All inclination in the illusion, the moving play or game,
towards unity and the realisation of unity
is the drawing power of Love.
At Mental and Physical levels,
the desire for union is experienced as the desire
for agreement and for physical love respectively;
at Causal level, it is experienced as Communion of Spirit.

In ignorance, Love degenerates into
the desiring to possess and identify
with that which appears to be the source of the love.
This possessive love admits duality,
the belief in another entity,
and thereby admits its complement, hate.
Possessive love is but a shadow of real Love, (*163*)
that which unifies all as One Existence, Communion.

Love should not be mistaken for possessive attachment
through identification,
the sentimental attachment of one for another,
especially that attachment that carries false obligation.
Perfect Love makes Perfect,
embraces all, allows no preferences, works in strange ways. (*164*)

For example, an adversary is commonly thought of
as one who is against 'me' and may be disliked or hated.
Adverse means 'turn towards'
and, in this context, an adversary
is one who may turn the mind towards understanding.
The overcoming of an adversary or of adversity
does not mean the defeating or destroying of him or it
but the transcendence of the duality
that has been caused by it in the mind,
the coming to realise the adversary or the adversity
as the opportunity to under-stand One Self, (*165*)
because the adversary or adversity is part of One Self.
The devil and his works are the resistance
that causes the discriminator to turn from ignorance, repent,
into the state of Love which is the Substance of One Mind.
It is not so much a case of 'loving thine enemies'
as 'loving thine enemies *as Thy Self*'.

Under-standing is Being *In* Love.
Love is a Substance; One is always *in* it.
It is ignorant to believe that One can be out of it.
The striving of 'one' to love 'another' is useless
since it generates and maintains the illusion of two.

'One' is always *in Love with* 'another'
though each may not realise it.
To believe each one separate is an illusion
arising from belief in each being the body-image
and, believing being separate from the beloved, denies Love.

Transcendence is to rise above the duality of separation
and there to express and experience Being In Love.
Such a state makes no demands, no preferences, (*166*)
for there is only One.
Without attachment and rejection there cannot be two.

It is an illusion to say "i love you";
nearer the Truth to say "i am in love with you";
truthful to say "I am in love"
because I AM is IN LOVE.
One *is* Love; One embraces All in Love.
One is Love,
Two is Creation, the product of Love,
Three is Resolution, the Realisation of Love,
the dissolving back to One, the Absolution of Sin (= Moon in Arabic).

To believe that 'me' or 'another' is the source of love
is an illusion;
each is a vehicle, or a mediator, for the drawing power of Love.
It is like thinking of the moon as a generating light source
when, in reality, it is reflecting the light of the sun.
To that degree is human love but a pale reflection
compared with the Source of Love.

Once there is the illusion of a separate 'me',
there is all the tension born of striving to change.
Once there is 'me' and 'other',
there is the illusion of love, hate, envy, greed, lust
and the disposition to violence and destruction.
The urge to violence is the urge to change,
to alter and mould all that which 'me' believes
is other than it ought to be.
The ignorant man resorts to violence;
the wise man works gently — hence, the gentle-man. (*167*)
The striving and worried man is a tortured, twisted man;
but the man who has abandoned belief in 'me' and 'mine',
in spite of and at the expense of 'others',
is a peaceful, dignified man,
dignified meaning worthy, worthy of being Man.

This is not to condone 'existentialism',
which is, in essence, the belief that since 'you' cannot change
anything, 'you' can do what 'you' like.
To come to such a belief is total ignorance
since it encourages total surrender to the belief
that a man is the body-image.
It results in apathy, irresponsibility and anarchy.
It is true that 'me' cannot change anything
since anything 'me' does is purely mechanical action and reaction;
but how it is seen and understood can change.

This principle is essential to understanding the One Philosophy;
'you' cannot change any thing;
but how it is seen can change
and that in itself brings about the change in things.

The second essential principle arising from this is that
the situation is always neutral;
it is the interpretation and re-action in the mind
that is significant. (*168*)

'You' cannot change anything means that the 'me',
the illusory separate self, cannot change anything, (*169*)
cannot change the laws that govern the forms of the physical world
in an attempt to make them lastingly perfect for that self.
But, by purification of the mental world,
a purgation that rids the mind of ignorant belief in 'me',
the sensorily perceived world becomes perfect
in that it is seen to be lawful, exactly and just as it should be.
It is *made* perfect *through* the eyes of the Beholder, the Self. (*170*)
The Self beholds all things to be Perfect
and thereby brings all things to Life.

What a man believes is the truth for him
and, if he believes that he is the body-image,
then he believes that when that image disintegrates, 'he' dies.
While he believes *in* death, and has a conception of what death means
then he will accordingly die.
Yet, seeing a dead body, where is that which had hitherto animated it?
It might be said "Where has life gone?"

Life cannot die; or it would not be Life.
If the Self is Realised to be the Animator, the Life,
that which animates the body, He cannot die. (*171*)

Sometimes men mourn the death of a man;
they sorrow because of *their* supposed loss.
They mourn in ignorance because they do not understand
what has happened. (*172*)
Do they think they can understand what it is like for him
who has died?
Who considers what has happened to the dead man?
Who considers the dead man?

Why assume that it is terrible to be dead?
The mourner projects himself into the imaginary situation
of being the other man, dead.
Being attached to the belief that he is the body,
he fears the cessation of all that with which
he has become identified.
Yet where did 'you' come from? Where do 'you' go?
The Self, what He is, comes from Nowhere and returns Nowhere. (*173*)
The Self is not born with the body
and does not die with the body.
When did 'you' begin?
The illusory 'me' arises and disappears
with the forming and the dissolving of the body-image.
When there is no longer held a belief *in* death,
there is no death. (*174*)

Why mental suffering and disease?
Mental suffering is the result of tension
caused by the continual striving to satisfy desire in the world, (*175*)

the continual wanting things to be other than they are,
the obstinate and tenacious holding of beliefs that are unreasonable and
the inevitable discomfort and disruption of disillusion.
Dis-ease, absence of ease,
is excessive and repeated tension in the body
caused by tension in the mind. (*176*)

These tensions cause imbalance in metabolic processes
rendering the body liable to internal or external agents
of disruption and destruction
The agents of these processes, viruses and bacteria for example,
are neutral;
they only seem good or bad from the viewpoint
of 'me' as the body-image.
In Nature, in the natural forming and dissolving process,
the excretory process is as important as the feeding process;
the breaking-down process is complementary to the building-up.
It is the Law of Nature that all things that have passed
their usefulness are destroyed or, better, transformed. (*177*)
It is all *just*; just as it is. (*178*)

War and fatal accident belong to the Causal realm of Mind, the gods,
and are related to the destiny of humanity and the particular being.
Until the Individual has Realised the illusion of death, (*179*)
He cannot understand the meaning of re-birth (*180*)
nor the meaning of Divine Justice and Divine Mercy.
In killing and being killed, Being transmigrates.

XXXVI *Space & Time*

The giving of identity,
the making entities of the things of the world,
includes identification with the body-image,
the creating of a false self.
Involved in the world, the mind measures in that world.
Since all things move, one form moving in relation to another,
there arise the concepts of distance and time.
These are useful as measurements in the physical world
but, from the point of view of the disengaged Self,
they are a super-imposition of no value.

When One appears to divide, to separate from Itself,
that which apparently stands between one and other,
subject and object, is called space.
The Self, in witnessing Itself, creates the apparent space, Mind.
Space is then a concept arising from the apparent separation
of one entity from another.
But what is space? Where is it?
These questions are meaningless because
how is it possible to locate, measure or describe
that in which all things are located, measured and described?
How much space does the Universe occupy?
Since there is One Universe as the sum total of All Things,
there can be no other against which it can be measured.
The Universe, to itself, is neither large nor small. (*181*)
The Universe has no size;
it is a dimensionless phenomenon in Mind.

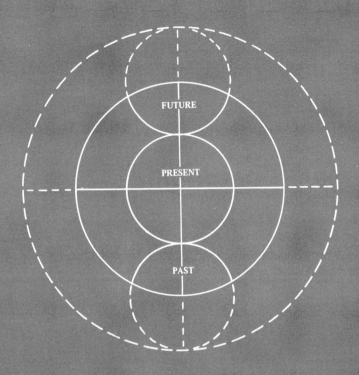

Likewise, chronological time is useful as measurement
of movement-duration in the Physical realm of mind.
Things move and change in relation to each other
and because these changing forms are impressed
in the memory substance of the Mental realm,
there arise the concepts of past and future.
The timelessness of memories and dreams is an indication
of the absence of time and space
when the Self is withdrawn from the senses.
The concept of past arises from the recall of previously witnessed images
and the concept of future is a projection of those recorded images
into an assumed continuation of chronological time.
The present is a dimensionless point, now.
In this dimensionless point, do past and future have real existence?
The commonly held model is that of past, present and future
as parts of a continuous 'straight line' time.(*182*)
Yet can the reality of the present
be in the same category as imagined past and future?
How long is the present?
No time at all; (*183*)
The present does not have duration
so how can the present begin and end?
Present is actual, now.
In reality, past, present and future are contemporaneous, (*184*)
related 'vertically', not 'horizontally'.
The future is the cause of what is now;
the present is being, here and now;
the past is what appears in the now. (*185*)

All Things in the sensorily perceived world are past;
for how can any thing take attention if it is not already there?
Any thing sensed in the moment now must already be created

otherwise it could not be there to be witnessed,
and, being already there, it is in the past.

Creation is the Past, being already created, (*186*)
which is why 'you' cannot change it.
The Present is the Witnessing in any given moment
of the Past being Presented.
The Future is that which causes the experience in the now.
The Self is the Witness in the Present
of the interaction of the Past and the Future,
of the Past becoming Future and the Future becoming Past. (*187*)

People continually want things to be other than they are;
it is useless wanting some thing or some situation
to be other than it is.
It is as it is
and 'you' cannot change the Past, Present or Future of this moment.
But, by Witnessing in the Present, in the Presence of the Self,
Knowledge brings about Evolution
ensuring that the Past will not have to repeat,
allowing the Ideal to come to Perfection.
It is not a case of 'you' trying to change the world
according to 'your' particular beliefs.
Wanting it to be as 'you' *think* it ought to be
is wilful, presumptuous and conceited.
But it is a case of allowing the Ideal to be Realised
willingly and without interference. (*188*)

Each human being called
by that still, quiet voice of Conscience (*189*)
comes to the estate of Manhood,
the state of Being In Love,
in which there is Realisation of the One Self.
The Being then becomes Realised
as truly indivisible, Individual.
And, as he forsakes the realm of Make-Believe,
He becomes Universal,
witnessing the Universe as Himself,
becoming totally Responsible.
Under-standing Will, standing under Law,
body and mind respond naturally to each moment
without thought as to how things ought or ought not to be (*190*)
because 'he', as a supposedly separate, particular being
no longer exists. (*191*)
There is Knowing Nothing.

The three important questions
"What is man?", "What is the universe?", "How are the two related?"
are resolved in the Realisation that
Man is Mind and contains the Universe as a reflection of Himself. (*192*)
The desires for knowledge, happiness and immortality
are seen to be one desire
which ceases in the Realisation that the Self, what One is, (*193*)
is Consciousness, which is Knowledge, which is Bliss.
There is then desiring Nothing, the Son returning to the Father.

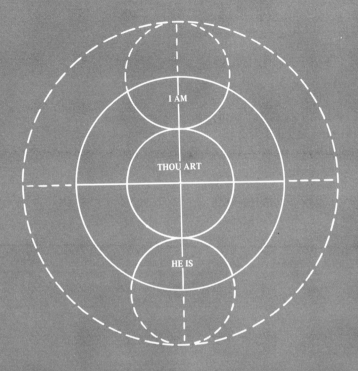

The acknowledgement I AM
disposes the mind to acknowledge THOU ART
by virtue of the creation HE IS

The caterpillar is a caterpillar is a caterpillar;
the butterfly is a butterfly is a butterfly;
one is not preferable to the other,
they co-exist eternally, now.
The acorn may or may not become an oak tree,
but, if destined to become an oak tree, it has no option. (*194*)
Of the millions of acorns each season only a few become oaks;
of the millions of human beings each generation,
only a few attain Manhood. (*195*)
When we are in the lower state, we aspire to the higher;
when in the higher, it is seen that there is no lower
and therefore that there is no higher either. (*196*)
Everything is Perfect
providing we have no opinion as to what perfection is.

Having Realised that 'a person' is not an independent entity with will
but a representation of forces and powers,
there are no people as constant, self-contained entities.
A man does not have a will to pursue particular aims
but he is a being through which universal forces work,
both creative and destructive,
the latter being as essential as the former
in the universal cycles of energy exchange,
the formation and disintegration of forms.
Thus no human being is to blame for his actions
not because he cannot help himself
but because *he is not*
until his season of coming to be.
Only the Individual is Responsible for His own Creation.
The means should never be mistaken for the end.

Because it is believed
that there is 'me' writing and 'another' reading,
or because it is believed
that there is 'me' speaking and 'another' listening,
there arises the illusion of duality. (*197*)

In Reality, there is simply and only
the appearance of written or spoken words,
the appearance of information.
The human being is formed as he is to be the vehicle for words
and it is through words as learning that he falls into ignorance.
But it is through words as the form of Knowledge
that he is raised again (*198*)
so that the One Self Realises Itself.

Transcending words,
before the Creation of the Word,
there is the silent Nothingness; (*199*)
which is why silence is said to be golden
and why
"all the rest is silence". (*200*)

In Other Words

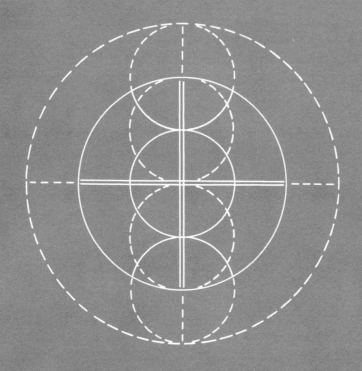

120

. . .I put it into thy mind to come up into this mountain, that thou mightest hear those things which it behoveth a disciple to learn from his teacher and a man from his God.

And having thus spoken, he showed me a cross of light fixed (set up), and about the cross a great multitude, not having one form; and in it (the cross) was one form and one likeness. And the Lord himself I beheld above the cross, not having any shape, but only a voice: and a voice not such as was familiar to us, but one sweet and kind and truly of God, saying unto me: John, it is needful that one should hear these things from me, for I have need of one that will hear. This cross of light is sometimes called the word by me for your sakes, sometimes mind, sometimes Jesus, sometimes Christ, sometimes door, sometimes a way, sometimes bread, sometimes seed, sometimes resurrection, sometimes Son, sometimes Father, sometimes Spirit, sometimes life, sometimes truth, sometimes faith, sometimes grace. And by these names *it is called* as toward men: but that which it is in truth, as conceived of in itself and as spoken of unto you, it is the marking off of all things, and the firm uplifting of things fixed out of things unstable, and the harmony of wisdom, and indeed wisdom in harmony. There are places of the right hand and the left, powers also, authorities, lordships, demons, workings, threatenings, wraths, devils, Satan, and the lower root whence the nature of things that came into being proceeded.

This cross, then, is that which fixed all things apart (or, joined all things unto itself) by the word, and separated off the things that are from those that are below, and then also, being one, streamed forth into all things (or, made all flow forth). But this is not the cross of wood which thou wilt see when thou goest down hence: neither am I he that is on the cross, whom now thou seest not, but only hearest his voice. I was reckoned to be that which I am not, not being what I was unto many others: but they will call me something else which is vile and not worthy of me. As, then, the place of rest is neither seen nor spoken of, much more shall I, the Lord thereof, be neither seen nor spoken of.

Now the multitude of one aspect that is about the cross is the lower nature: and they whom thou seest in the cross, if they have not one form, it is because not yet hath every member of him that came down been comprehended. But when the human nature (or, the upper nature) is taken up, and the race which draweth near unto me and obeyeth my voice, he that now heareth me shall be united therewith, and shall no more be that which now he is, but above them, as I also now am. For as long as thou callest not thyself mine, I am not that which I am:

but if thou hear me, thou, hearing, shalt be as I am, and I shall be that which I was, when I have thee as I am with myself. For from me thou art that which I am. Care not therefore for the many, and they that are outside the mystery despise; for know thou that I am wholly with the Father, and the Father with me.

Acts of John

I

1 Like the bee gathering honey from different flowers, the wise man accepts the essence of different Scriptures and sees only the good in all religions.

Srimad Bhagavatam

2 The deepest truth cannot, like other objects of study, be put into words: from long intercourse and close intimacy with the facts, it comes suddenly into existence in the soul, like a light kindled by a flying spark, and at once becomes self-supporting.

Plato

3 The Mandala, or "magic circle", is a "uniting symbol" which, according to Jacobi, first appears "when the process of individuation nears its end, that is, when the inner psyche is experienced as just as real, just as effective and psychologically true, as the world of outer reality. The appearance of this symbol, which represents an archetype of the psychic totality (ie. of the 'self') always shows a more or less abstract form of representation because a symmetrical ordering of parts and their relation to a central point constitutes its laws, thus bringing out its essence. The Orient has known such symbolic representations from early times." . . . . . according to Jacobi, it indicates "the highest goal of psychic development, the self".

II

4 For many are called, but few are chosen.

Matthew

5 The highest function of man's soul is the perception of truth.

Al-Ghazzali

6 While in the Dharma itself there is no individuation.
They ignorantly attach themselves to particular objects.
It is their own mind that creates illusions.
Is this not the greatest of all Self-contradictions?

Seng-Ts'an

7 Our self-seeing There is a communion with the self restored to its purity. No doubt we should not speak of seeing, but of seen and seer, speak boldly of a simple unity. For in this seeing we neither see nor distinguish nor are there two. The man is changed, no longer himself nor self-belonging; he is merged with the Supreme, sunken into It, one with It; only in separation is there duality. This is why the vision baffles telling; for how could a man bring back tidings of the Supreme as detached, when he has seen it as one with himself? It is not to be told, not to be revealed to any who has not had the happiness to see. . .Beholder was one with beheld. . .he is become the Unity, having no diversity either in relation to himself or anything else. . .reason is in abeyance and intellection, and even the very self, caught away, God-possessed, in perfect stillness, all the being calmed. . .This is the life of gods and of godlike and blessed men — liberation from the alien that besets us here, a life taking no pleasure in the things of the earth — a flight of the alone to the Alone.

Plotinus

III

8 And when the Oneness is not thoroughly understood
In two ways loss is sustained;
The denying of reality is the asserting of it
And the asserting of emptiness is the denying of it.

Seng-Ts'an

9 If thou dost desire to approach this abode of immortality, and to attain to this exalted station, divest thyself first of self and then summon to thyself a winged

123

steed out of nothingness to bear thee aloft. Clothe thyself with the garment of nothingness and drink the cup of annihilation. Cover thy breast with a nothingness, and draw over thy head the robe of non-existence.

Attar

10 He who sees the Infinite in all things sees God. He who sees the Ratio only sees himself only. Therefore God becomes as we are, that we may be as He is.

William Blake

11 Image — reflection, appearance, representation; c.f. imago — the final and perfect stage after all metamorphoses, e.g. the butterfly.

IV

12 The disciples said unto Jesus: Tell us how our end will be. Jesus said: Have you then discovered the beginning so that you enquire about the end? For where the beginning is, there shall be the end. Blessed is he who shall stand at the beginning, and he shall know the end and he shall not taste death.

Gospel according to Thomas

13 If they ask you: What is the sign of your Father in you?, say to them: It is a movement and a rest.

Gospel according to Thomas

14 The absoluteness of truth implies the relativity of all formulations of it.

Radhakrishnan

15 The mystery of life is not a problem to be solved, it is a reality to be experienced.

J. van der Leeuw

V

16 'I don't know what you mean by "glory", ' Alice said.
Humpty Dumpty smiled contemptuously. 'Of course you don't — till I tell you. I meant "there's a nice knock-down argument for you!" '
'But "glory" doesn't mean "a nice knock-down argument," ' Alice objected.
'When *I* use a word,' Humpty Dumpty said in rather a scornful tone, 'it means just what I choose it to mean — neither more nor less.'
'The question is,' said Alice, 'whether you *can* make words mean so many

different things.'

'The question is,' said Humpty Dumpty, 'which is to be master — that's all.'

Lewis Carroll

17 The world as it appears to common sense consists of an indefinite number of successive and presumably causally connected events, involving an indefinite number of separate individual things, lives and thoughts, the whole constituting a presumably orderly cosmos. It is in order to describe, discuss and manage this common-sense universe that human languages have been developed. Whenever, for any reason, we wish to think of the world, not as it appears to common sense, but as a continuum, we find that our traditional syntax and vocabulary are quite inadequate.

Aldous Huxley

18 Though we are conscious of a three-dimensional world, we still think in terms of a two-dimensional logic, based on the law of identity and non-identity, ie. having only two alternative directions: 'either this *or* that'. It was the realisation of this deficiency in every-day language and thought that led Nâgârjuna, the great Buddhist philosopher of the 2nd century AD., to an entirely new approach towards the spiritual problems of human life and to the discovery of new dimensions of consciousness. This led to a negation of all philosophical or conventional concepts and to the use of paradoxes in hinting at experiences which go beyond conceptual thought, until a new language had been found, in which the experiences of meditation and inner vision were reflected, a language 'beyond the path and usage of the philosophers', which is devoid of all predicates, such as being and non-being, oneness and otherness, bothness and non-bothness, existence and non-existence, eternity and non-eternity.

Lama Anagarika Govinda

19 Truth is within ourselves; it takes no rise
Fom outward things, whate'er you may believe.
There is an inmost centre in us all
Where the truth abides in fulness; and around,
Wall upon wall, the gross flesh hems it in,
This clear perfection which is truth.
A baffling and perverting carnal mesh
Binds it, and makes all error; and to know
Rather consists in opening out a way
Whence the imprisoned splendour may escape,
Than in effecting entry for a light
Supposed to be without.

Robert Browning

20 Is that a wonder?
   The providence that's in a watchful state
   Knows almost every grain of Pluto's gold;
   Finds bottom in th' uncomprehensive deeps;
   Keeps place with thought, and almost, like the gods,
   Does thoughts unveil in their dumb cradles.
   There is a mystery — with whom relation
   Durst never meddle — in the soul of state;
   Which hath an operation more divine
   Than breath or pen can give expression to.

Shakespeare

21 The Self is not realisable by study nor even by intelligence and learning. The Self reveals its essence only to him who applies himself to the Self. He who has not given up the ways of vice, who cannot control himself, who is not at peace within, whose mind is distracted, can never realise the Self, though full of the learning of the world.

Katha Upanishad

22 Seek in the Impersonal for the Eternal Man.

The Buddha

VI

23 But I say unto you, That every idle word that men shall speak, they shall give account thereof in the day of judgement. For by thy words shalt thou be justified, and by thy words shalt thou be condemned.

Matthew

24 Faith is verification by the heart.

Sufism

25 The truth indeed has never been preached by the Buddha, seeing that one has to realise it within onself.

Sutralamkara

26 With means that are inconstant I have obtained that which is constant.

Katha Upanishad

27 It is worth noting that the first five verses of St. John's Gospel are in the past tense except the first part of the fifth verse which is in the present tense.

VII

28 For some must watch, while some must sleep;
So runs the world away.

Shakespeare

29 The gods. . .allot to each individual his appropriate destiny, one that is in
harmony with his past conduct, in conformity with his successive existences.
Such Things as happen to the good without justice, as punishments, or poverty,
or disease, may be said to take place through offences committed in a former
life.

Plotinus

30 For, as he thinketh in his heart, so is he.

Proverbs

31 Therefore is the name of it called Babel; because the Lord did there confound
the language of all the earth; and from thence did the Lord scatter them abroad
upon the face of all the earth.

Genesis

32 Jesus said: Let him who seeks not cease seeking until he finds, and when he finds
he will be troubled, and when he has been troubled, he will marvel and he will
reign over the All.

Gospel according to Thomas

VIII

33 Remember how long thou hast been putting off these things, and how often
thou hast received an opportunity from the gods, and yet dost not use it. Thou
must now at last perceive of what universe thou art a part, and of what
administrator of the universe thy existence is an efflux, and that a limit of time is
fixed for thee, which if thou dost not use it for clearing away the clouds from
thy mind, it will go and thou wilt go, and it will never return.

Marcus Aurelius

34 Man's life on earth has only one end and purpose: to identity himself with the
eternal Self and so come to unitive knowledge of the Divine Ground.

Aldous Huxley

IX

35 'Ignorant' is not essentially a derogatory term. There is no stigma attached to being ignorant any more than being human. It is an inevitable phase in evolution.

36 The intoxication of life and its pleasures and occupations veils the truth from men's eyes.

Jalalu'd-din Rumi

37 He said to them: You test the face of the sky and of the earth, and him who is before your face you have not known, and you do not know to test this moment.

Gospel according to Thomas

38 Those abiding in the midst of ignorance, self-wise, thinking themselves learned, running hither and thither, go around deluded, like blind men led by one who is himself blind.

Katha Upanishad

39 But, when one knows the creatures in God, that is called and is 'morning knowledge'; and in this way one sees the creatures without any differentiation and stripped of all images and deprived of all similarity in the One, who is God Himself. This also is the nobleman of whom our Lord said: 'A nobleman went out'. He is noble because he is one, and because he knows God and creatures in the One.

Eckhart

40 He who wants to obtain true faith must know, because faith grows out of spiritual knowledge. The faith that comes from that knowledge is rooted in the heart.

Paracelsus

41 The skill which souls derive from experience is sufficient to their salvation.

Plotinus

42 Only as I know a thing myself, do I know it.

Kwang Tse

43 Look thou to My Face and turn from all save Me; for My Authority is eternal and shall never cease; My Kingdom is lasting and shall not be overthrown.

Baha-u-llah

X

44 Ye fools and blind: for whether is greater, the gift or the altar that sanctifieth the gift?

Matthew

XI

45 For knowledge in effect is to know a thing as it is in itself and not as it is reputed to be.

Komensky

46 Are not all your ideas borrowed from your senses, which do not give you the reality but only its phenomena?. .For absolute truth is not to be found in the phenomenal world.

Eckhart

47 When we return to the root, we gain the meaning;
When we pursue the external objects, we lose the reason.
The moment we are enlightened within,
We go beyond the voidness of the world confronting us.

Seng-Ts'an

XII

48 Transformations going on in an empty world that confronts us
Appear all real because of ignorance:
Try not to seek after the true,
Only cease to cherish opinions.

Seng-Ts'an

49 For things Divine are not accessible to mortals who fix their minds on body; 'tis they who strip them naked that speed aloft unto the Height.

Chaldean Oracles

50 In taking knowledge of an object, the soul suffers defect of unity, and is not wholly one; for knowledge is an account of things, and an account is manifold, and so our soul lapses into number and multiplicity, and misses the One.

Plotinus

51 We are unable to understand that Existence is not our private property, that it is universal and absolute...The superimposition of the ego-idea upon existence is our first and most important idea as human beings. The moment we have made this central act of superimposition — the moment we have said "I am I, I am private, I am separate, I am individual", we have made further superimposition inevitable.

Phenomena do not arise independently but rely upon environment. And it is their appearing as objects which necessitates all sorts of individualised knowledge. You may talk the whole day through, yet what has been said? You may listen from dawn till dusk, yet will you have heard? Thus, though Gautama Buddha preached for forty-nine years, in truth no word was spoken.

Huang Po

52 Verily I say unto you, Whosoever shall not receive the Kingdom of God as a little child, he shall not enter therein.

Mark

53 The great man is one who has never lost the heart of a child.

Mencius

54 All old tales such as fairy tales, involving imprisoned or sleeping heroines (eg. princesses) being rescued by heroes (eg. princes), refer to the release from ignorance by Knowledge.

55 Three things prevent a man from knowing God. The first is time, the second is corporeality, the third is multiplicity. That God may come in these things must go out — except thou have them in a higher, better way; multitude summed up to one in thee.

Eckhart

56 Perfection is attained, not when there is nothing more to add, but when there is nothing more to discard.

St. Exupéry

57 As fire is the direct cause of cooking, so Knowledge, and not any other form of discipline, is the direct cause of liberation; for liberation cannot be attained without Knowledge.

Action cannot destroy ignorance, for it is not in conflict with ignorance. Knowledge alone destroys ignorance, as light destroys dense darkness.

It is because of ignornace that the Self appears to be finite. When ignorance is destroyed, the Self which does not admit of any multiplicity whatsoever, truly reveals Itself by Itself, like the sun when the cloud is removed.

Atmabohda

58 But the Kingdom is within you and it is without you. If you will know yourselves, then you will be known and you will know that you are the sons of the Living Father. But if you do not know yourselves then you are in poverty and you are poverty.

Gospel according to Thomas

XIII

59 The claim to individuality for ourselves implies individuality everywhere. It automatically superimposes a multiple world of creatures upon the one, undivided reality, the existence which is Brahman. Ego-idea and world-appearance depend on each other. Lose the ego-idea in transcendental consciousness, and the world-appearance must necessarily vanish.

Swami Prabhavananda

60 Demand not things to happen as you will, but will them to happen as they do happen and you will live in peace.

Epictetus

XIV

61 No action, as such, is either good or bad; but its character depends on how it is performed.

Plato

62 A very ridiculous thing it is, that a man should dispense with vice and wickedness in himself, which it is in his power to restrain; and should go about to suppress it in others, which is altogether impossible.

Marcus Aurelius

Why beholdest thou the mote that is in thy brother's eye, but considerest not the beam that is in thine own eye?

Matthew

63 Meddle not with many things, if thou wilt live cheerfully. Certainly there is nothing better than for a man to confine himself to necessary actions. Another man's sin. Why should it trouble thee? Let him look to it, whose sin it is.

Marcus Aurelius

64 This above all — to thine own self be true;
And it shall follow as the night the day,
Thou canst not then be false to any man.

Shakespeare

XV

65 Cast away from thee opinions, and thou art safe.

Marcus Aurelius

66 Understanding is the reward of faith. Therefore do not seek to understand in order that you may believe, but make an act of faith in order that you may understand; for unless you make an act of faith, you will not understand.

St. Augustine

67 He to whom the eternal word speaks is set at liberty from a multitude of opinions.

Thomas à Kempis

XVI

68 All that we are is the result of what we have thought; it is founded on our thoughts, it is made up of our thoughts.

Dhammapada

69 Man is made by his belief. As he believes, so he is.

Bhagavad-Gita

70 Depend not on another, rather lean upon thyself, trust to thine own exertions.

Laws of Manu

XVII

71 Without beginning thou embracest all, for by thee are all the worlds created.

Svetasvatara Upanishad

72 That which is the finest essence — this whole world has that as its soul. That is reality. That is Atman. That art thou.

Chandogya Upanishad

73 The light of the body is the eye: if therefore thine eye be single, thy whole body shall be full of light.

Matthew

74 It (the One) is in reality ineffable. . .of that which is beyond all things, it is alone true to assert that it has not any other name. . .Properly speaking, however, there is no name of it, because nothing can be asserted of it.

Plotinus

75 If only men could see that there is nothing to do, nothing to achieve, nothing to claim, in this already complete and blissful creation.

Shankaracharya

76 Were the earth to become paper, the forest pens, and the wind a writer, the end of the endless could not be described.

Arjan

77 God created man to be immortal, and made him to be an image of his own eternity.

Wisdom of Solomon

78 Lord Shri Krishna said: "This impenetrable philosophy I taught to Viwaswāna the founder of the Sun-dynasty, Viwaswana gave it to Manu the Lawgiver, and Manu to King Ikshwàku!
The Divine Kings knew it, for it was their tradition.
Then after a long time, at last it was forgotten.

The Geetà

79 Life's but a walking shadow; a poor player
That struts and frets his hour upon the stage,
And then is heard no more: it is a tale
Told by an idiot, full of sound and fury,
Signifying nothing.

Shakespeare

[This reveals perhaps not so much despair as realisation.]

80 In spiritual affairs the man is always more important than the tribe or state, or that vague entity 'mankind'. All doctrine which elevates the state at the expense of the individual is evil; it reverses the current of good. The well-trained individual man, woman or child, is the only true objective of civilisation, for a nation of such is the ideal state. A developed and independent man is of more use to the nation than a frightened slave, and the worship of the concept of state is to create a devil within whose grasp the flower of spirit dies.

Christmas Humphreys

81 Then with the lapse of years, the truth grew dim and perished. . .Knowledge is darkened by ignorance, and mankind becomes deluded.

Bhagavad-Gita

XVIII

82 The importance of the creation of the ZERO mark can never be exaggerated. This giving of airy nothing not merely a local habitation and a name, a picture, but helpful power, is the characteristic of the Hindu race from which it sprang. . .No single mathematical creation has been more potent for the general on-go of intelligence and power.

G. P. Halstead

83 In the Great Beginning there was nothing; nothing that could be named. In this state rose the first existence, but without concrete form; and from this things could then be produced. This can be described as spiritual power at work. The formless then came to be divided.

Kwang Tse

84 There was something, undefined and complete, coming into existence before Heaven and Earth. How still it was and formless, standing alone and undergoing no change, reaching everywhere and in no danger of being exhausted. It may be regarded as the Mother of all things.

Lao Tse

85 All things under Heaven sprang from Tao as existing; that existence sprang from Tao non-existent.

Lao Tse

86 Were there not this unborn, unoriginated, uncreated, unformed, there would be no escape from the world of the born, originated, created, formed.

The Buddha

87 At the advent of Brahma's day all manifested things are produced from the unmanifested.

Bhagavad-Gita

88 In this world, being is twofold: the Divided, one: the Undivided, one. All things that live are "the Divided". That which sits apart, "the Undivided".

Bhagavad-Gita

XIX

89 Thou must love God as not-God, not-Spirit, not-person, not-image, but as He is, a sheer, pure, absolute One, sundered from all two-ness, and in whom we must eternally sink from nothingness to nothingness.

Eckhart

90 No man can serve two masters.

Matthew

91 Thou shalt not take the name of the Lord thy God in vain.

Exodus

XX

92 Jesus said unto them, Verily, verily, I say unto you, before Abraham was, I am.

John

93 The change from being to becoming seems to be birth and the change from becoming to being seems to be death, but, in reality, no one is ever born, nor does one ever die.

Apollonius of Tyana

94 For as long as thou callest not thyself mine, I am not that which I am; but if thou hear me, thou, hearing, shalt be as I am, and I shall be that which I was, when I have thee as I am with myself.

Acts of John

XXI

95 What is is the same as what is not,
What is not is the same as what is:
Where this state of things fails to obtain,
Indeed, no tarrying there.

Seng-Ts'an

96 He who thinks that God has any quality and is not the One, injures not God, but himself.

Philo of Alexandria

The nought here mentioned is God, to whom the soul may be united when she is nowhere bodily, nor hath in her any image of creatures. And when she is nowhere bodily then she is everywhere spiritually; and being in such condition she is fit to be united with the said nothing which also is in all places. In reality this is a union of spirits, of the man's spirit with God's spirit, there being in neither of them any bodily image or thing. And this union I have elsewhere called a union of nothing with nothing.

Commentary on The Cloud of Unknowing

98 The man who claims that he knows, knows nothing; but he who claims nothing, knows.

Upanishads

99 When my Beloved appears, with what eye do I see Him? With His Eye, not with mine, for none sees Him except Himself.

Ibn Al Arabi

XXIII

100 The interpreter or messenger, Mercury or Hermes.

101 When Mind and each believing mind are not divided,
And undivided are each believing mind and Mind,
This is where words fail:
For it not of the past, present and future.

Seng-Ts'an

102 The Cross on Golgotha will never save thy soul:
The Cross in thine own heart alone can make thee whole.

Angelus Silesius

XXIV

103 Jesus said: If they say unto you: "From where have you originated?", say unto them: "We have come from the Light, where the Light has originated through Itself. It stood and it revealed itself in their image".

Gospel according to Thomas

104 cf. Greek legend of Narcissus.

105 Jesus said: Whoever has known the world has found a corpse, and whoever has found a corpse, of him the world is not worthy.

Gospel according to Thomas

106 Having established noblest reason as a charioteer, from on high, and when, having put aside thy body, thou comest into the free aether, thou shalt be deathless, a god imperishable, no longer mortal.

Golden Verses of the Pythagoreans

107 Vanity of vanities, saith the Preacher, vanity of vanities; all is vanity. What profit hath a man of all his labour which he taketh under the sun?

Ecclesiastes

108 All that in Adam fell and died, was raised again and made alive in Christ, and all that rose up and was made alive in Adam, fell and died in Christ.

Theologia Germanica

XXV

109 When you have understood the destruction of all that was made, you will understand that which was not made.

Dhammapada

110 Things are indifferent, but the uses of them are not indifferent.

Epictetus

111 Jesus said: Become passers-by.

Gospel according to Thomas

112 Accept not because it is in the scriptures, by mere logic, nor by consideration of appearances. . .But, if at any time you know of yourself "these are sinful conditions, these are wrongful. . .", then eschew them.

Anguttara-Nikaya

113 Verily I say unto you, Inasmuch as yet have done it unto one of the least of these my brethren, ye have done it unto me.

Matthew

XXVI

114 If a beginning were created from anything, it would not be a beginning. *Plato*

115 I am the beginning and the end. *Apocalypse of John*

XXVII

116 When the end has been restored to the beginning, and the termination of things compared with their commencement, that condition of things will be re-established in which rational nature was placed, when it had no need to eat of the tree of good and evil.

Origen

117 I entered into my inmost soul and beheld even beyond my light and soul the Light Unchangeable. He who knows the truth knows what that Light is and he knows It knows eternity. Thou art love! And I beheld that Thou makest all things good, and that to Thee there is nothing whatever evil.

St. Augustine

118 And the Lord commanded the man, saying, Of every tree in the garden thou mayest freely eat: But of the tree of the knowledge of good and evil, thou shalt not eat of it: for in the day that thou eatest thereof thou shalt surely die.

Genesis

119 To a good man nothing is evil.

Plato

120 Men are liable to sin. . .from the time they are made capable of understanding and knowledge, when the reason implanted within has suggested to them the difference between good and evil; and after they have already begun to know what evil is, they are made liable to sin, if they commit it.

Origen

121 All such actions (selfless) belong to what is known as ethical goodness — just as all selfish actions belong to ethical evil. In one sense, and in one sense only, may goodness be said to be more 'real' than evil: since evil actions and thoughts involve us more deeply in maya, while good actions and thoughts lead us beyond maya, to transcendental consciousness.

The words sin and virtue are somewhat alien to the spirit of philosophy, because they necessarily foster a sense of possessiveness to thought and action. If we say 'I am good' or 'I am bad', we are only talking the language of maya. I am Brahman (Absolute) is the only true statement regarding ourselves that any of us can make. . .We must never forget that ethical conduct is a means, not an end in itself. Knowledge of the impersonal reality is the only valid knowledge. Apart from that, our deepest wisdom is black ignorance and our strictest righteousness is all in vain.

Swami Prabhavananda

122 But I say unto you, That ye resist not evil. . .

Matthew

123 *Phiroz Mehta*

124 God is to be enjoyed, creatures only used as means to That which is to be enjoyed.

St. Augustine

125 Nothing in excess.

Carved on the temple to Apollo at Delphi

126 Let your moderation be known unto all men.

St. Paul

XXVIII

127 These our actors,
    As I foretold you, were all spirits, and
    Are melted into air, into thin air:
    And, like the baseless fabric of this vision,
    The cloud capp'd towers, the gorgeous palaces,
    The solemn temples, the great globe itself,
    Yea, all which it inherit, shall dissolve,
    And, like this unsubstantial pageant faded,
    Leave not a rack behind. We are such stuff
    As dreams are made on; and our little life
    Is rounded with a sleep.

Shakespeare

128 When the more exalted parts of us energise, and the soul is elevated to natures better than itself, then it is entirely separated from things which detain it in generation.

Iamblichus

129 For whosoever hath, to him shall be given, and he shall have more abundance: but whosoever hath not, from him shall be taken away even that he hath.

Matthew

(cf. also Matthew: 'But seek ye first the kingdom of God, and his righteousness: and all these things shall be added unto you.' These references to those that 'hath' and 'hath not' are to those who have realised the Self and those who have not.)

130 It is better to do one's own task, though imperfectly, than to do another's even though well-performed.

Bhagavad-Gita

131 All the world's a stage
And all the men and women merely players;
They have their exits and their entrances;
And one man in his time plays many parts,
His acts being seven ages.

Shakespeare

[The last sentence may be taken to refer to re-birth and the seven stages of development in evolution.]

132 When you strive to gain quiescence by stopping motion,
The quiescence thus gained is ever in motion;
As long as you tarry in the dualism
How can you realise Oneness?

Seng-Ts'an

133 In order to arrive at having pleasure in everything,
Desire to have pleasure in nothing.
In order to arrive at possessing everything,
Desire to possess nothing.
In order to arrive at being everything,
Desire to be nothing.
In order to arrive at knowing everything,
Desire to know nothing.

St. John of the Cross

134 Pleasure is only an illusion of happiness, a shadow of happiness, and in this delusion man perhaps passes his whole life, seeking after pleasure and never finding satisfaction. . .The one who is happy is happy everywhere: in a palace or a cottage, in richness or poverty, for he has discovered the fountain of happiness which is situated in his own heart. . .Happiness cannot be bought or sold, nor can you give it to a person who has not got it. All religions, all philosophical systems, have taught man in different forms how to find it. . .And wise men have in some form or another given a method. . .and have called this process 'alchemy'. . .A person who follows a religion and has not come to the realisation of truth, of what use to him is his religion if he is not happy? A religious person must be happier than one who is not religious.

Al-Ghazzali

140

135 Hamlet's soliloquy "To be or not to be. . .", in its esoteric sense, presents the choice as to whether it is nobler to accept the reality of the sensorily perceived world and all that goes with such belief or whether to aspire to the full consciousness which requires the 'death' of the illusory self.

136 And Adam said, This is now bone of my bones, and flesh of my flesh: she shall be called Woman, because she was taken out of Man.

Genesis

137 Jesus said to them: When you make the two one, and when you make the inner as the outer and the outer as the inner and the above as the below, and when you make the male and the female into a single one, so that the male will not be male and the female [not] the female. . .then shall you enter [the Kingdom].

Gospel according to Thomas

XXIX

138 Be still, and know that I am God.
Psalms

139 It is the mind which gives to things their quality, their foundation and their being.
Dhammapada

140 If you expect to gain anything from teachers or other doctrines, what is your purpose in coming here? So it is said that if you have the merest intention to indulge in conceptual thinking, behold, your very intention will place you in the clutch of demons. Similarly, a conscious lack of such intention, or even a consciousness that you do NOT have NO such intention, will be sufficient to deliver you into the demons' power. But they will not be demons from outside; they will be the self-creations of your own mind. The only reality is that 'Bodhisattva' whose existence is totally unmanifested even in a spiritual sense — the Trackless One. If ever you should allow yourself to believe in the more than purely transitory existence of phenomena, you will have fallen into a grave error known as the heretical belief in eternal life; but if, on the contrary, you take the intrinsic voidness of phenomena to imply mere emptiness, then you will have fallen into another error, the heresy of total extinction.

Huang Po

XXX

141 Jesus said: I am the Light that is above them all, I am the All, the All came forth
from Me and the All attained to Me. Cleave a (piece of) wood, I am there; lift up
the stone and you will find Me there.

Gospel according to Thomas

142 Attention is the only path the Buddhas ever trod.

143 Pondering on objects of the sense there springs attraction; from attraction grows
desire; from desire is produced passion; from passion comes delusion; from
delusion results obscuration of memory.

Bhagavad-Gita

144 Such things as enter from without will never cease to flow in as long as there is
no resolution to control the receptivity – the wishes, intentions and desires.

Huai Nan Tse

145 Man has the power of self-control, and no external influences can control him if
he exercises this power.

Paracelsus

146 Let us, then, labour for an inward stillness –
An inward stillness and an inward healing;
That perfect silence where the lips and heart
Are still, and we no longer entertain
Our own imperfect thoughts and vain opinions
But God alone speaks in us, and we wait
In singleness of heart, that we may know
His will, and in the silence of our spirits,
That we may do His will, and do that only.

Longfellow

147 When are liberated all the desires that lodge in one's heart, then a mortal
becomes immortal. Therein he reaches Brahma.

Katha Upanishad

XXXI

148 To be free from repulsion and attraction, or from the wish to take or avoid – to
enter into the mood of complete impartiality – is the most profound of arts.

Tibetan Book of the Dead

149 Present fears
Are less than horrible imaginings.
My thought, whose murder yet is but fantastical,
Shakes so my single state of man, that function
Is smothered in surmise; and nothing is
But what is not.

Shakespeare

150 For now we see through a glass, darkly; but then face to face.

St. Paul

151 Excessive pleasures and pains are what we should deem the greatest disease of
the soul; for when a man is over-elevated with joy or unduly depressed with
grief, and so hastens immoderately either to retain the one or fly from the other,
he can neither perceive nor hear anything properly, but is agitated with fury, and
very little capable of exercising the reasoning power.

Plato

152 The spirit of man loves purity, but his mind disturbs it.
The mind of man loves stillness, but his desires draw it away.
If he could always send his desires away, his mind would of itself become still.
Let his mind be made clean, and his spirit will of itself become pure.

Khing Kang King

XXXII

153 Truth is the science of wisdom preserved in memory by conscience.

Book of Dwyfyddiaeth

154 It would be better to have no books than to believe everything in books.

Mencius

155 Let the counsel of thine own heart stand: for there is no man more faithful to
thee than it.

Ecclesiasticus

156 Consciousness is the sole basis of certainty. . .Knowledge has three degrees —
opinions, science, illumination. The means or instrument of the first is sense; of
the second, dialectic; of the third, intuition.

Plotinus

XXXIII

157 The Father is made of none: neither created nor begotten.
The Son is of the Father alone: not made, nor created, but begotten.
The Holy Ghost is of the Father and the Son: neither made, nor created, nor begotten, but proceeding. . .

The Creed of St. Athanasius

158 Jesus said to her (Salome): I am He who is the Same, to Me was given from the things of My Father.
Salome said: I am Thy disciple.
Jesus said to her: Therefore I say, if he is the Same, he will be filled with light, but if he is divided, he will be filled with darkness.

Gospel according to Thomas

159 Wherefore I say unto you, All manner of sin and blasphemy shall be forgiven unto men: but the blasphemy against the Holy Ghost shall not be forgiven unto men.

Matthew

XXXIV

160 The ways are two: love and want of love. That is all.

Mencius

161 The desire and pursuit of the whole is called Love.

Plato

162 In One and with One is the beginning and origin of blossoming and fervent love. One is the beginning without any beginning. Similarity is the beginning from the One alone, and it receives what it is, and the fact that it is a beginning, from and in the One. Love has the property of flowing and springing from Two as One. One as unity does not give love; two as duality does not produce love; two as one naturally gives willing, fervent love.

Eckhart

163 Ambiguity in vocabulary leads to confusion of thought; and, in this matter of love, confusion of thought admirably serves the purpose of an unregenerate and divided human nature that is determined to make the best of both worlds — to say that it is serving God, while it is in fact serving Mammon, Mars or Priapus.

Aldous Huxley

164 Let me not to the marriage of true minds
   Admit impediment. Love is not love
   Which alters when it alteration finds,
   Or bends with the remover to remove:
   O, no! it is an ever-fixed mark, . . .

Shakespeare

165 Those who speak ill of me are really my good friends.
   When, being slandered, I cherish neither enmity nor preference,
   There grows within me the power of love and humility,
   Which is born of the Unborn.

Kung-chia Ta-shih

166 The perfect way knows no difficulties
   Except that it refuses to make preferences;
   Only when freed from hate and love
   It reveals itself fully and without disguise;
   A tenth of an inch's difference
   And heaven and earth are set apart.

Seng-Ts'an

XXXV

167 The characteristic of Tao is gentleness.

Lao Tse

168 If therefore it be a thing external which causes thy grief, know that it is not
   properly that which doth cause it, but thine own conceit and opinion concerning
   the things which thou mayest rid thyself of, when thou wilt.

Marcus Aurelius

169 Which of you by taking thought can add one cubit to his stature?

Matthew

170 For we know in part, and we prophesy in part.
   But when that which is perfect is come, then that which is in part shall be done
   away.

Corinthians

171 If an ordinary man, when he is about to die, could only see the five elements of
   his consciousness as void; the four physical elements as not constituting an 'I';
   the real Mind as formless and neither coming nor going; his nature as something
   neither commencing at his birth nor perishing at his death, but as a whole and

motionless at its very depths; his Mind and environmental objects as one — if he could really accomplish this, he would receive Enlightenment in a flash.

Huang Po

172 In the sight of the unwise they seemed to die: and their departure is taken for misery, and their going from us to be utter destruction: but they are in peace.

Wisdom of Solomon

173 Those would I teach, and by right reason bring to think of death as but an idle thing. Why thus affrighted by an empty name?. . .nor dies the spirit, but new life repeats in other forms, and only changes seats.

Pythagoras

174 O Friend, hope for Him whilst you live, know whilst you live,
understand whilst you live; for in life deliverance abides.
If your bonds be not broken whilst living, what hope of deliverance in death?
It is but an empty dream that the soul shall have union with Him because it has passed from the body;
If He is found now, He is found then;
If not, we do but go to dwell in the City of Death.

Kabir

175 Whatever pain arises is all in consequence of craving; but from the complete destruction of craving, through absence of passion, there is no origin of pain.

The Buddha

176 To set up what you like against what you dislike —
That is the disease of the mind:
When the deep meaning (of the Way) is not understood,
Peace of mind is disturbed to no purpose.

Seng-Ts'an

177 There is no coming-into-existence without destruction; there is no destruction devoid of origination; neither origination nor destruction can truly be without stability.

Pravacana-sara

178 Nothing therefore of the things which they will say of me have I suffered; nay, that suffering also which I showed unto thee and the rest in the dance, I will that it be called a mystery. For what thou art, thou seest, for I showed it to thee; but what I am, I alone know, and no man else. Suffer me then to keep that which is mine, and that which is thine behold thou through me, and behold me in truth, that I am, not what I said, but what thou art able to know, because thou art akin thereto. Thou hearest that I suffered, yet did I not suffer; that I have suffered not, yet did I suffer. . .

Acts of John

179 The whole of nature is that book which the soul is reading. Each life, as it were, is one page of that book; and that read, it is turned over, and so on and on, until the whole of the book is finished, and the soul becomes perfect, having got all the experience of nature. Yet at the same time, it never moved, nor came nor went; it was only gathering experiences.

But it appears to us that we are moving. The earth is moving yet we think that the sun is moving instead of the earth, which we know to be a mistake, a delusion of the senses. So is also this delusion that we are born and that we die, that we come or that we go. We neither come nor go, nor have we been born. For where is the soul to go? There is no place for it to go. Where is it not already?

Swami Vivekananda

180 A stone I died and rose a plant,
   A plant I died and rose an animal;
   I died an animal and was born a man;
   Why should I fear? What have I lost by death?

Jalalu'd-din Rumi

XXXVI

181 Infinitely small things are as large as large things can be,
   For no external conditions obtain;
   Infinitely large things are as small as small things can be,
   For objective limits are here of no consideration.

Seng-Ts'an

182 Past and future veil God from our sight;
   Burn up both of them with fire.
   How long wilt thou be partitioned by these segments like a reed?
   So long as a reed is partitioned, it is not privy to secrets,
   Nor is it vocal in response to lip and breathing.

Jalalu'd-din Rumi

183 The highest part of the Soul starts above time and knows nothing of time. In eternity there is neither time nor space, neither before nor after; everything is present in one fresh-springing Now.

Eckhart

184 I am Yesterday, To-day, and To-morrow.

Egyptian Book of the Dead

185 That which has been is that which shall be. . .and there is no new thing under the sun.

Ecclesiastes

186 He who sees what now is, hath seen all that ever hath been from times everlasting, and that shall be to eternity.
There is nothing that is new.

Marcus Aurelius

187 The scriptures say: "Before the created world I am". He says "Before I am". That is, when man is raised up above time into eternity, he works there one work with God. Some people ask how man can do the works that God did a thousand years ago and will do a thousand years hence, and they do not understand it. In eternity, there is neither "before" nor "after". For this reason, what occurred a thousand years ago and will do a thousand years hence and what happens now, are all one in eternity. . . And this is for wise people a matter of knowledge and for the ignorant a matter of belief.

Eckhart

188 Thy Will Be Done.

The Lord's Prayer

XXXVII

189 The present condition of the world is diseased. If I were a doctor and was asked for my advice I should answer create silence, bring men to silence — the word of God cannot be heard in the world today. And if it is blazoned forth with noise so that it can be heard even in the midst of all other noise, then it is no longer the word of God. Therefore create silence.

Kierkegaard

190 Be satisfied with your business, and learn to love what you were bred to; and as to the remainder of your life, be entirely resigned, and let the gods do their pleasure.

Marcus Aurelius

191 But what is true obedience? I answer, that a man should stand so free, being quit of himself, that is of his I, and Me, and Self, and Mine, and the like, that in all things he should no more seek or regard himself than if he did not exist, and should take as little account of himself as if he were not and another had done all his works. Likewise he should count all the creatures for nothing. What is there then which is and which we may count for somewhat? I answer, nothing but that which we may call God.

Theologia Germanica

192 He who knows what Man is, rests in the knowledge of the known, waiting for the unknown.

Kwang Tse

193 A man must become truly poor and as free from his own creaturely will as he was when he was born. And I tell you, by the eternal truth, that so long as you *desire* to fulfil the will of God and have any hankering after eternity and God, for just so long you are not truly poor. He alone has true spiritual poverty who wills nothing, knows nothing, desires nothing.

Eckhart

194 To every thing there is a season, and a time to every purpose under the heaven. . .

Ecclesiastes

195 For many are called, but few are chosen.

Matthew

196 A master was asked the question: "What is the Way?" by a curious monk.
"It is right before your eyes."
"Why do I not see it for myself?"
"Because you are thinking of yourself?"
"What about you? Do you see it?"
"So long as you see double, saying 'I don't' and 'You do' and so on, your eyes are clouded," said the master.
"When there is neither 'I' nor 'You', can one see it?"
"When there is neither 'I' nor 'You', who is the one who wants to see it?"

Zen story

197 Essential to the mystical experience is the suspension, or obliteration, of the subject-object distinction; in other words, an immediate assurance of the consubstantiality of knower and known. Since normal cognition presupposes the distinction, and language reflects normal cognition, the experience is, as every mystic has testified, ineffable: "What can be shown cannot be said".

Wittgenstein

198 So shall my word be that goeth forth out of my mouth: it shall not return to me void, but it shall accomplish that which I please, and it shall prosper in the thing whereto I sent it.

Isaiah

149

199 When a man hath finished, then he is but at the beginning.

Ecclesiasticus

200 We shall not cease from exploration
And the end of all our exploring
Will be to arrive where we started
And know the place for the first time.

T.S. Eliot